I0127686

The Monkey's Tail

In the 1960s T. C. Lethbridge's challenging, probing studies were well established. First published in 1969, *The Monkey's Tail* was as remarkable as his previous investigations. Mr Lethbridge – who was trained in Natural Science before he became an archaeologist – had for years been unable to accept Darwin's theory of Evolution. In this book he examines the theory in the light of his observations and experience. He found it wanting in every particular which he examined.

In the first part of the book Mr Lethbridge puts his case against the theory of Evolution, and in the second part he shows that the known facts of Evolution could be equally well explained in another way. He had for many years been working on the 'fringe' study of Extra Sensory Perception, and he used that study to present an alternative theory to Darwinism.

Mr Lethbridge was well aware that much more evidence was needed before his ideas could either be proved or disproved finally; but they do provide a reasoned explanation based on years of careful study. The theory he put forward was not only more compatible with observed scientific fact at the time, but less at variance with accepted religious beliefs.

This book is a re-issue originally published in 1969. The language used is a reflection of its era and no offence is meant by the Publishers to any reader by this re-publication.

The Monkey's Tail

A Study in Evolution and Parapsychology

Tom Lethbridge

Routledge
Taylor & Francis Group

LONDON AND NEW YORK

First published in 1969
by Routledge & Kegan Paul

This edition first published in 2025 by Routledge
4 Park Square, Milton Park, Abingdon, Oxon, OX14 4RN

and by Routledge
605 Third Avenue, New York, NY 10017

Routledge is an imprint of the Taylor & Francis Group, an informa business

© 1969 Tom Lethbridge

Publisher's Note
The publisher has gone to great lengths to ensure the quality of this reprint but points out that some imperfections in the original copies may be apparent.

Disclaimer
The publisher has made every effort to trace copyright holders and welcomes correspondence from those they have been unable to contact.

A Library of Congress record exists under ISBN: 0710065981

ISBN: 978-1-032-94360-2 (hbk)
ISBN: 978-1-003-57033-2 (ebk)
ISBN: 978-1-032-94370-1 (pbk)

Book DOI 10.4324/9781003570332

The monkey's tail

A study in evolution and parapsychology

Tom Lethbridge

London

Routledge & Kegan Paul

First published in 1969
Routledge & Kegan Paul Ltd
Broadway House, 68–74 Carter Lane
London, E.C.4

Printed in Great Britain
by C. Tinling & Co. Ltd
London and Prescot

© *Tom Lethbridge 1969*

SBN 7100 6598 1

List of figures

Introduction

For much of my life at Cambridge I was a student of the Dark Ages—that period long ago when the rule of Rome slowly fell to pieces. It is impossible to look about the world today without observing many of the same symptoms and this compels me to try to see whether there may not be some way in which this miserable process could be reversed.

The root of the trouble seems to lie in a false philosophy, which is directly due to a faulty interpretation of the Theory of Evolution. If all life is assumed to be governed by chance alone, how can man be expected to conform to a code of morality, which interferes with his own particular pleasures and advancement? However if it can be shown that the theory is wrong and there is good evidence that everything is planned from outside, then it becomes necessary to think again.

The purpose of this book is to make a limited investigation of the current theory and, when this appears to fail in many important details, to put forward some suggestions as to what might really have taken place and may be taking place now.

This involves an intensive investigation of matters which are scarcely regarded as worth noticing by orthodox science, but which are obviously capable of exact and serious study. When this is undertaken, as my wife and I have been doing for the last ten years or so, such an entirely different state of affairs is revealed that it is necessary to go back to the beginning and revise all the ideas on which so much education and training is now employed. Orthodox science has cut itself off from investigating these things with its own self-imposed terms of reference, and only the very boldest, such as Sir Alister Hardy and Raynor Johnston, dare to step over the barrier.

The barrier is due to the assumption that man has only five senses, while it is evident that he really has at least six. If everything has to be judged against sight, hearing, touch, taste and smell, then you leave out such matters as can be appreciated without the use of any of these faculties. For instance memory is one which everybody admits and yet nobody can measure.

I will say no more on this now and leave the reader to judge for himself whether I am writing sense or not; but if he finds himself in agreement with only a part of what I have to say, then a door to a different world will open for him.

Throughout these investigations my wife has been of the greatest help to me. She has the gift of an incisive mind and can see straight through to the root of a problem, which would often take another person weeks of concentrated thought to solve. It is, of course, another form of the operation of the sixth sense. We come to the same conclusions about matters which we at first regarded with complete disbelief; but it is a great help to have her confirmation and it also sharpens one's wits. She too has had the boring task of typing out the manuscript and getting the tables in order. My thanks cannot be stated in words.

Part One

One

The western shore of the Outer Hebrides is unique. On the eastern side, facing the Highland mainland, you might be anywhere on the west of northern Europe; but the opposite coast, only a few miles away, has a distinctive atmosphere which seems to be derived from the great Atlantic Ocean itself. It is, I think, fair to say that it has been built by the Western Ocean out of the wreckage of the land behind it and that the sea is slowly claiming its own again. Much sentiment has been poured out in books; but I have never seen it discussed as a fascinating geological and topographical study, nor has much attention been given to the various ancient peoples who settled on its flat and luxuriant meadowland and succeeded one another without even their names being known.

Of course the trouble was that sixty miles of the stormy Minches have to be crossed and that the mail boats are small and somewhat uncomfortable. The possibility of some hours of sea-sickness is a considerable deterrent to the normal run of scholars. So to most of Britain the beauty of the *machair* on the edge of the Western Ocean remained unknown till aeroplanes began to arrive in the north of Benbecula, where once I used to lie up in the sand dunes to watch the grey-lag geese, or searched for pins and pottery in the middens around Iron Age wheel-houses buried in the sand. Five of these wheel-houses are said to have been destroyed in the construction of the Benbecula airport. It is not known what people made them; but, since the Outer Islands were known to the geographer Ptolemy as Dumna, it seems probable that they were a branch of the tribe known to the Romans as Damnonii, or Dumnonii, who were also found in Roman times about the Clyde and in the west of England as well.

Although this book is not intended as an antiquarian study, these wheel-house people were the accidental cause of it and are so interesting that I feel that it is worth spending a little time in talking about them, even if most of the talk is speculation.

At least four thousand years ago the Outer Islands were well known to the people who built the great stone monuments of western Europe.

Who these seafaring people were is as much unknown as ever it was. But a recent theory suggests that they built a kind of observatory at Callernish in Lewis as a check-point for calculating eclipses, and subsidiary to Stonehenge. That anybody should go to such trouble suggests that the people who made it came from a highly organized and maritime civilization somewhere much further south than Britain. That the islands at that time were sufficiently fertile and attractive to support a considerable population is attested by the huge chambered burial-cairns, known as *bharpa*, which are found here and there down the island chain. But the spectre of sea-sickness kept them out of the ken of most of the archaeologists who write learned works about the megaliths of western Europe, and even the efforts of the late Sir Lindsay Scott, who found the actual settlements of the people, did little to disperse the ignorance.

All the traces of this early civilization are on an old land surface, which was evidently reasonably fertile at the time; but something happened to the general pattern of climate and the west of Scotland as a whole became intensely wet. Almost the whole of the islands was slowly covered by a blanket of peat which ruined the land, crept up the stones of Callernish and concealed smaller monuments completely. In Eriskay I have seen a whole group of Bronze Age burial-cairns, recently rediscovered when the peat was removed for fuel. In short, some five or six hundred years before the birth of Christ the Outer Islands and much of the west mainland of Scotland became almost uninhabitable, and the population vanished. The effect of the climatic change was felt all over the ancient world. Angry, starving tribes started to migrate in search of somewhere else to live. Once started, these migrations and attendant wars continued for more than a thousand years. At some time around the birth of Christ the people we are thinking of as the Damnonii discovered that there were many miles of fertile grazing land on the west of the Outer Hebrides. 'Hebrides' is, in itself, an ancient name displaced from its original location. The Aebudoi were evidently that group of islands which extends northwards from Kintyre to Mull. The Malaeus of the Aebudoi is in fact the present island of Mull. The Outer Islands were known as Dumna as I have already noted.

The grazings on the west of Dumna were at least twice as wide as they are today. The land has been sinking slowly since that time and in many places you can see the freshwater peat beds of the Bronze Age at least three feet below modern high-tide level. This has happened all over the west coast. In Canna harbour, for instance, a ring of stones now known as Sgeir a bharpa (the reef of the burial-cairn) is completely covered at high-tide. Assuming that the name refers to a prehistoric burial and not to an Iron Age house, this shows clearly how much the land has sunk in about 3,500 years. I actually saw the ring of stones showing above the tide from high up in the Canna hills and told John Campbell, the author and Gaelic scholar, who owns the island. He was quite unwilling to believe what I had seen until he found that the place name still existed. Of course, most of the stones have been removed at some time or other to build the croft houses on the shore behind. This is the common fate of ancient monuments. Handy, usable stone is removed to build houses, dykes or roads. It is far less trouble to rob an older building than to crack up hard rock with fire and water.

The skeleton of the Outer Islands is a blunted saw of old, folded, igneous rock, sloping steeply to the east and more gently to the west. Against the western slope of this chain of hills the sea has spread miles of wide sandy flat. This was once the bed of the ocean at a time when there was more water in the sea than there is today. Between the hills and the plain there are dozens of small lakes formed in the hollows of the bedrock itself. These lochs and lochans are famous for their trout and often made beautiful with white water-lilies. On Loch Bee, at the north end of South Uist, the surface is covered with white dots, the famous wild swans which even today are more or less sacred, for of course they are princesses magically transformed.

On to this meadow land, the *machair*, which smells like honey in summer, and where corncrakes still make a deafening din and fly about like untidy partridges, came the men who built the wheel-houses somewhere about the time that Christ was born. They were nomadic and they were seafarers. I suppose it would be fair to call them Celts, for their culture was much the same as that of the earlier Celtic Iron Age in southern Britain; but who they were really and where they came from we do not know.

On the flat *machair* these newcomers set up their round leather tents, and to protect them from their animals they built a concentric ring of domed, stone store-chambers, like the spokes of a wheel without the hub. Outside this again was a narrow passage enclosed by another stone wall. The stones were all set in fire-clay instead of mortar, a custom also found in some early Roman buildings in the west of England. On a central hearth within the leather tent burned a fire of dried peat, and peats were stored in some of the stone chambers. The entrance passage passed out through all the walls and faced the fire.

The origin of this curious type of homestead was, I feel certain, one of timber, although the central leather tent was fundamental. It was

7

the normal dwelling of Ireland, so the gypsies say, right down till the eleventh century after Christ. The outer rings developed for protection from wind and animals. Cows always rub against buildings and a leather tent would not stand it. The inner faces of the piers of the surrounding store-chambers were carefully graded and shaped by mauls to fit the curve of the leather. They stood at least ten feet high.

Unless I am much mistaken the stone walls were an absolute necessity, for it seems clear that these men tamed and imported the red deer into the Outer Islands. The distance is too great for a breeding stock ever to have swum across the Minch. The minute red deer of North Uist which, except for occasional deliberate importations, can obviously never have had any fresh blood for centuries, are survivors from the herds of the wheel-house people. So I think are the deer on Rum.

Let us look at their name for a moment. Ptolemy calls them the Damnonii or Dumnonii. Actually the name ends in 'oi', for it has been translated from Latin into Greek. Like all the names in Ptolemy's geographical tables this has been so frequently copied in manuscript that it is distorted. I think this name was originally Damnonii and that it meant 'the people of the Stag'. If it was Dumnonii then it perhaps means 'the people of the World'; but 'stag' seems more likely. There were other peoples in Celtic Britain known by the names of their tribal totems; cats, cows and horses at least are clear. These totems remained right on into the Dark Ages and are probably to be seen in the heraldic arms still borne today. It is also remarkable that out of the mass of pottery recovered from the rubbish heaps of the wheel-house people only two fragments are ornamented with free-hand drawings. Both are of stags.

For perhaps three hundred years the Damnonii remained as herdsmen in the Hebrides, and then another climatic change seems to have overtaken them. The Greenland and Arctic Ice Caps must have started to melt again and the sea to rise. Evidence for this is to be found in other places. Holland began to flood and extensive Romano-British settlements in the English fens were seriously affected. The more exposed *machairs* were eaten into, and sand-dunes started to move inland over the peoples' houses.

This was ruinous for most of the islanders and they moved on once more. Some may have remained until the Norse settlements of the eighth century, but the majority put their leather tents into their boats and set out again. I think they went in two directions, some to the lowlands of Scotland and others to Donegal and Mayo, although for the latter journey I have no more than a hint in the Irish story of the Children of Lir. But we will hear more of this later, for the wheel-house people were, I think, magicians, and their former dwellings are known as *sithean* (*sheean*), or fairy hills, to this day.

In the summer of 1951 we went across the Minch in our boat, *old Zoraida II*, and let go in the only corner of Lochboisdale harbour where there is a reasonable chance that one's anchor won't be pulled straight through the mud by the first gale which comes along. This is a minute, rock-encircled hole below the police station. It is so small that I have come back to the boat at low-tide to find her just afloat in a tiny pool of water, which would have held no second boat of any kind. Our intention was to visit the middens of the wheel-house people on the *machair* at Daliburgh and Kilpheder. I had known at least five middens there and visited them from time-to-time during the last twenty-five years. Beneath the Daliburgh graveyard a wheel-house had been destroyed to build the churchyard wall. It was known as Sithean a Phiobaire, the piper's fairy hill. Objects from its midden, which still remained, seemed to date from the first century after Christ. But it was in the dunes beyond Kilpheder, where there were at least three middens, that we had a stroke of good fortune. There had been a spell of fine weather with prolonged dry wind. At one point near a midden, where the dunes were covered by short grass, we found the circumference of a ring, some thirty feet across, where the roots had died from want of moisture. It was obvious that there was a circular wall beneath the turf and that in all probability this was a wheel-house. A test-hole landed us in one of the cells round its edge and the walls were still standing to a height of 8 ft. This is what I had been hoping to find for many years, and so arrangements were made to excavate it the following year.

In the summer of 1952 we dug out the wheel-house. It was in such good order that it must have filled up with sand soon after its people left. Small objects were still in crannies in the walls, and a fine, enamelled Roman brooch lay on the shelf of a bee-hive alcove in the back wall. The house was, in fact, such a good specimen that four years later when the Queen visited the islands I was asked to come over to show it to her. I told her I thought she must be the first queen ever to see the inside of a fairy hill and she appeared to take considerable interest in it.

But shifting sand is hard work. It is far heavier than ordinary earth. We often took a rest and walked down to the sea which was only a hundred yards or so away. There you look southwards to the distant hills of Barra or westward over drowned lands; two churches are said to be beneath the waves, with nothing but a lobster boat between you and America (fig. 1). This is the real 'Rim of the World', as it has been described in Gaelic song.

9

Figure 1 Kilpheder beach, South Uist, Barra in distance. Grey seals on reef in middle distance, often there.

Strange things wash up on Kilpheder sands; beans from the West Indies, *Entada gigas* and *Muncana urens*, known respectively as Mary's bean and Mary's kidney, which are held to be charms in childbirth, and other dangers: coconuts, glass net-floats, American electric-light bulbs and an occasional Portuguese man-of-war. But on 11th July, after a succession of south-westerly gales, we found the tide-mark covered with small objects which looked like dried skins off people's thumbs. Their texture was much like that of the cast skin of a snake. We had no idea what they were, till at last we found a perfect specimen preserved in a pool of water. It was a small, flat jelly-fish of greenish-blue colour with a purple-blue edging. Tentacles hung beneath it and on top it had a triangular, membranous sail set diagonally to its longer axis (fig. 2.1). It was not till we returned to Cambridge that it was identified for us as *Velella spirans* or, in English, By-the-Wind-Sailor. For, incredible as it may seem, this little ocean organism does sail into the wind, if it is not altogether too violent.

This apparently trivial piece of information was enough to start me on a train of thought which has completely changed all my fundamental ideas about natural history and the world in which we live. Much of my time throughout the years has been spent in the study of ancient shipping and navigation. I have even written books on the subject: *Boats and Boatmen* and *Coastwise Craft*. To me, sailing into the wind, as opposed to running before it, was a great and difficult art which man did not learn until thousands of years after he became a

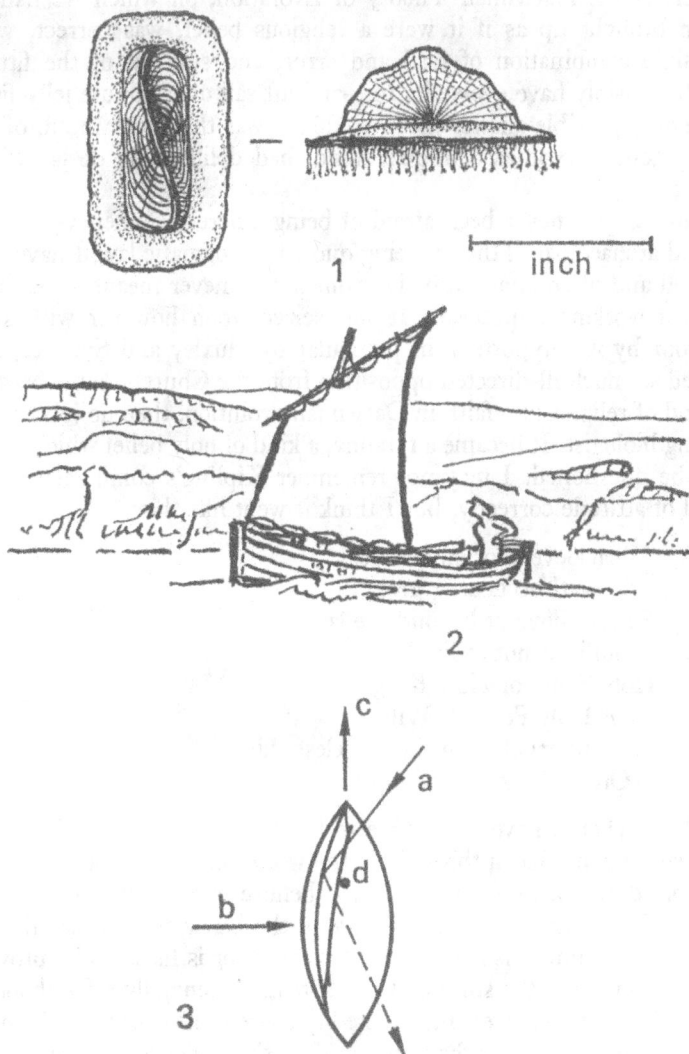

Figure 2 'By-the-Wind' sailors. 1. *Velella* jelly-fish. Dotted area vivid blue. 2. Lug-sail boat sailing into the wind. North bay, Barra. 3. Pressures on a lug-sail boat: (*a*) wind on sail; (*b*) pressure of the water; (*c*) direction of boat's movement; (*d*) mast.

sailor. If the Darwinian Theory of Evolution, on which we had all been brought up as if it were a religious belief, was correct, what possible combination of trial and error, and survival of the fittest, could possibly have evolved a fore-and-aft sail on a minute jelly-fish? The only possible answer that I could see was that some mind, of the same general type as a human mind, had deliberately designed the thing.

Now I have never been afraid of being a heretic. Whenever I have found archaeological theory being quoted as dogmatic law, I have suspected and often attacked it. Darwinism was never meant to be more than a working hypothesis. It was seized upon however with such fervour by its supporters, in particular by Huxley and Spencer, and raised so much ill-directed opposition from the Church that it became a kind of religion: no faith in Darwinian evolution, then no job for the young biologist. It became a tyranny, a kind of holy belief which could not be questioned. I may not remember Kipling's comment on this kind of attitude correctly, but I think it went like this:

> 'Whatsoever, for any cause,
>   Seeketh to take or give
> Power above or beyond the laws,
>   Suffer it not to live!
> Holy State, or Holy King—
>   Or Holy People's Will—
> Have no truck with the senseless thing.
>   Order the guns and kill!'

And this should have been done to the Darwinian theory, for it has caused immense harm throughout the world for too long a time.

That does not mean that I do not believe in evolution as such. Of course I do. But I no longer believe in the Darwinian explanation of it. I do not think this has ever been proved, or is likely to be proved, for it is only half the story and a half-truth is generally a falsehood. I think Darwin deserves much credit, shared of course with A.R. Wallace, for the theory they produced on the evidence they had at the time. But all the same, readers must remember that Darwin was warned by his Cambridge professor, Adam Sedgwick, that if he persisted in publishing this theory it would wreck the world and utterly debase mankind. The older man knew what he was talking about. The theory, as narrowed and enforced by Spencer and Huxley, has very nearly wrecked the world. Without it Marxism would never have got the hold it has, and Freud would not have formulated his somewhat degrading theories. For it set a premium on sex and greed.

The 'survival of the fittest' meant that anyone who thought he was a specimen of the fittest, one of the *Herrenvolk*, could stamp on the faces of everybody else. It also meant that, since the development of the world was governed by chance and there was nothing else to account for it, you therefore had to use your short life to the best of your own advantage, and to tramp over anyone who stood in your path.

Of course Darwin himself never meant this. He had a bright idea and all the available facts of the time seemed to support it. Nevertheless, if there was anything in the prophesy of the coming of Antichrist, he fulfilled it. The theory took God right out of the picture. Mankind in future reverted to the animal side of his nature and became 'red in tooth and claw'—at least a large part did. We have been paying for our too easy acceptance of the theory ever since.

Jelly-fish are a most complicated and difficult study. What appears to be a single organism, a jelly-fish to the ordinary person, is considered to be, in reality, a colony of individual organisms known, quaintly enough, as 'persons'. These persons are of two kinds, a feeding individual, often provided with poisonous stinging tentacles, and a reproducing individual, a medusa, formed like a bell. The early stages of the persons, who later form the colony of a single jelly-fish, are often completely unknown. Of course all creatures are in a sense colonies; but in jelly-fish the union of complete organisms is more obvious.

The family to which the By-the-Wind-Sailor belongs is known as the *Siphonophora*. The simplest form of this is a kind of straight tube, with the individual persons of each kind branching out from it. At the end of this tube there is a kind of bubble-like bulge, full of gas, and known as a phenocyst. This acts as a float and keeps the whole colony at an even depth in the water. It was the development of this phenocyst, in itself not easily explained by any form of trial and error on the part of the jelly-fishes, which ultimately formed the basis of the By-the-Wind-Sailor's sail.

Jelly-fish as a race live by netting their food out of the sea with their tentacles, which are often several feet long and highly poisonous as well. The best known of the *Siphonophora* on our shores is *Physalia physalia*, the Portuguese Man-of-War, which has poisonous tentacles many feet long and is dangerous to bathers. Its phenocyst, which keeps the whole colony afloat, has become a kind of elongated and crested bladder which, when left high and dry on the beach, looks not unlike a decaying, translucent sweetbread some 8 inches long and of a pale blueish colour shot with pink. While most jelly-fish are at the mercy of the ocean currents for transport and can only move by opening and shutting their bowl-shaped cover, the Portuguese Man-of-War adds the chance of wind to blow it across the surface of the water. This is an important advantage to a catcher of fish, for it enables it to sweep a larger area of sea than can a non-wind-driven jelly-fish. But still it can only fish down wind. The By-the-Wind-Sailor goes considerably further and by sailing at an angle to the wind covers fresh areas of water all the time. The whole process is remarkably similar to that once performed by the trawlers of Brixham or Lowestoft, which sailed into the wind towing their trawl nets after them. One can see that the apparatus for the evolution of *Velella* was already available in *Physalia* and that the drying-up and hardening of part of the bladder float could have produced *Velella's* sail at an angle to the longitudinal axis of the animal in such a way that the pressure of the wind and drag of the tentacles would send the colony at an angle to the direction of the wind. This is precisely the way in which a sailing vessel beats to windward (fig. 2.3).

Now all this information, except perhaps the details of the construction of jelly-fish, was available in the days of the great Darwinian controversy of the 1860s. Why did no one mention it? The answer must be that it was a war of specialists. Both churchmen and scientists had been familiar with sailing vessels all their lives. There were no internal combustion engines. All progress on the sea in small vessels was by sail and oar. But a sailor was thought of as an ignorant, lower-class being, even if Nelson, Howe and Hood, Prince Rupert, Charles II and his brother James had belonged to that fraternity. James had even been saved from the shipwreck of a man-of-war in the North Sea; but what of that? It was a long time ago. 'As to jelly-fish—nonsense! We are dealing with the higher animals and the ancestry of god-like man himself.' No one is known to have said that; but it is the way they went on. And if you confine your quarrels to the so-called higher animals, of course they are red in tooth and claw, for that is the manner in which many of them were designed to live. It should have been obvious, however, that the primates, the great apes, were more or less vegetarian and rather peaceful and easy-going in their habits. If they were in the ancestral line of man, then it was clear that he did not attain his position by his superiority in killing his animal neighbours. But why should this puzzle be confined to the higher animals. It must obviously include all animals and all plants too.

Evolution concerns all living things. If the survival of the fittest concerns lions, whales and giraffes, it also concerns worms, roses and bacteria. What is the fittest? Is a sparrow-hawk, which lives by killing small birds, fitter and higher on the scale of evolution than the infinitely more numerous sparrows and chaffinches on which it preys? Are the warrior tribesmen of the hills fitter, or less fit, than the crowded and often near-starving millions of the plains of India? Which will survive longer? It seems to me to be entirely a matter of personal opinion which living things you decide to be the fittest. Yet geological study shows plainly that innumerable species of animals have been evolved and then have died out; while in the botanical field we can watch the spread of some plants until they completely smother others which were successfully growing there before. There obviously is a struggle for existence; but is the battle fought out in the apparent way, or is it not perhaps one in the minds of beings higher than ourselves who are continually designing and experimenting with forms of living creatures? This possibility was entirely left out in the Victorian evolutionary war, because the scientists were unable to think in terms of more than five senses and three dimensions; while the churchmen were still governed by the theories and beliefs of more than a thousand years before. There was no common ground on which they could meet and talk things over. Neither side was right, as is usually the case with wars, and nothing will be right until both sides of the picture are studied as a whole. As we go on I hope to show how the subject could be tackled by more able persons than I. Just to set people thinking is something in itself. I cannot hope to prove things, for it would take much hard work by many people to do so. But I can throw stones into the pool of complacency and get a few people here and there to think matters out for themselves. This is not a case for specialized knowledge along one narrow line, but of general knowledge, observation and reasoning from facts. It is no good just stuffing facts into a computer and saying: 'This is the answer!' A computer is useless unless the correct facts are fed into it. It is at the mercy of the person who provides the facts, and, judging by what happens in many fields today, the intelligence of the fact-providers is often not of a high order. An excellent example of this occurred at Honiton recently. Honiton, on the main road to the west; is a market town with a wide main street, which has ample room for shoppers to stop their cars and do their business. But at the northern end there was a bad bottle-neck, which often caused lengthy congestion to the through traffic. So, at vast expense and with considerable difficulty, a fine new by-pass was constructed and opened with pride by the Minister of Transport. Then the town's inhabitants woke to the realization that 'no parking' lines had been painted on both sides of the main street, which effectively closed their shops to all commerce. A cry of indignation arose and representations were made to the Ministry to find why, now that all through traffic passed outside the main street, this folly had been perpetrated. They were told that a computer had provided this answer.

Obviously some ignorant person had fed the wrong facts into it. Readers will be glad to know that the lines were removed and Honiton has returned to its normal life again. But computers will always be liable to give the wrong answers in inverse proportion to the mental ability of the person who feeds them with facts. At times the answers may be very strange indeed.

If then we take a general look at the world of nature, picking out examples here and there, we are more likely to get correct answers than if we take one branch and study it in detail. If our general examination seems to tell us that Darwinian evolution does not explain what we see, then we shall have to look around for another explanation. There is little to be gained in only destroying a theory. In that process much else is often lost. Our object must be to provide if possible some other idea which does work.

Two

As a child I picked up from somebody a rhyme which has a lot of sense in it. Probably I did not learn it correctly, but what I remember is this:

> The cod-fish lays ten thousand eggs, the homely hen but one;
> But the cod-fish never cackles to proclaim her work is done.
> Wherefore we spurn the cod-fish coy; the friendly hen we prize.
> Which really only goes to show it pays to advertise.

Nowhere in nature is so much murder done as in the sea. From the acorn-barnacle living in its tiny fortress on a rock and sweeping its nets for diatoms, to the voracious killer whale, there are few inhabitants of the ocean who are not born to kill. Here, surely, the rule of the survival of the fittest should be obvious. The most stream-lined and determined hunter ought to sweep the board. But, if you look at it all from a wide angle, the hunters seem to prey to a large extent on smaller hunters and leave less drastic forms, who live on organisms much lower in the scale than themselves, to grow to an enormous size and prosper till man takes a hand in the story. The basking shark feeds on plankton and grows to a weight of several tons. The walrus, the largest northern member of the seal family, lives on shell-fish and the whale-bone whales filter relatively minute, naked snails and other tiny creatures through their baleen sieves.

Of course man has upset the balance. He has almost exterminated the northern baleen whales. He has seriously reduced the number of walrus and he has made a start on the basking and Arctic sharks. I must say that having looked down from the deck of my boat on to the monstrous forms of basking sharks I find them singularly repulsive; but walrus, whether sitting on an ice floe or a rock, or swimming in the sea, have a charm of their own. I do not know whether they 'sing' like the grey ocean seals do on the skerries of the Outer Islands, but I should be quite prepared to hear that they do. The weird calling of the grey seals in the distance, when there are several together, cannot fail to make you think of a male voice choir, in some Cambridge college chapel, heard across the Backs. I have never seen a right whale, the true whale-bone whale, for they were practically exterminated before the First World War. However I have seen the larger fin whales and within perhaps twenty-five yards too. Their size is so great that from a small vessel they are quite alarming.

Now these three beasts in themselves are enough evidence for us to look on the evolutionary theory of the survival of the fittest in the face of bloody competition with at least some suspicion, for most of their comparatively near relations are carnivorous. We have to assume from this theory that they grew to this large size because they flourished on their less carnivorous diet to a greater extent than the other members of their orders. The baleen whales were more successful than the killer whales. The plankton-feeding sharks were more successful than the carnivorous sharks and the shell-fish-eating walrus more successful than the fish-eating seals. Furthermore, if we turn away from the sea for a moment, we find a similar picture on land. The largest and in some ways to man the most dangerous land animals, the elephant, the rhinoceros and the buffalo, are herbivorous. They did not attain their position by killing off their rivals. As a boy I knew several big-game hunters. Without exception they placed the wild buffalo as the most dangerous beast to hunt. It stalked the stalker. The great apes too, the gorilla, orang-outang, and chimpanzee, although they will eat grubs and small animals, are to a large extent vegetarian, and not aggressive creatures. The most we seem to be able to say in favour of the theory at this stage is that certain predators such as the cat family manage to support themselves very well on a carnivorous diet, although we must add that they certainly have never succeeded in exterminating the animals on which they feed, for this would have entailed their own demise.

We are not dealing with mammals, however, at the moment. Let us get back to fish. To all appearances the shark family is a very primitive one. Its skeletons are said not to be bones like those of other fish, but only cartilage. Its senses are so weakly developed in some respects that when specimens have been caught from ships, hauled on board and disembowelled with the casual brutality of uninformed sailors and thrown overboard alive, the same eviscerated sharks have been soon caught again on hooks baited with their own guts. Yet sharks small or great swarm in every sea; dog-fish, skates and rays are all members of this primitive family. They have not been driven from the seas by more highly developed fishes.

It is only an assumption that cartilagenous fish preceded bony fishes in geological time; but if they did so, as seems most probable, then numerous later and more elaborate developments were no more successful. You can go to a chalk pit and dig out the teeth of sharks which lived perhaps two hundred million years ago and are hardly distinguishable from those of sharks living today. The teeth are the only part that is likely to be preserved. Had there been toothless cartilagenous fish far back in past ages, it is improbable that we should know anything about them.

Now if the cartilagenous type of fish was so successful, what pressure of natural selection produced the bony-skeletoned fish, which not only failed to oust the more primitive type, but never produced forms of such vast size as the basking and whale-headed sharks? The basking shark moreover feeds not on the flesh of other fish, but on minute plankton. And so, if you lean over the rail of a boat to see the grotesque and rather repulsive monstrous shape of a basking shark swimming unhurriedly beneath you, you are looking at a type which was a success so long ago that our minds are quite unable to appreciate this vast period of time. That success was apparently due to the simplicity of its diet and not to any rivalry whatsoever.

When we turn to the bony fishes we are at first liable to be awed by the vast range and variety. But once again it is evident that very early types were such a success that their descendants are known to this day. Everyone remembers the surprise and even shock which were caused to zoologists when coelacanths began to be caught off Madagascar in recent years. These comparatively large fish had been supposedly extinct for two hundred million years. This demonstrated that the geological record is in reality only a sketch of what must have been, and at the same time showed how much remains to be learnt about what is living in the sea.

However, for a long time science has been aware that bony fishes of the earliest known types were still living in the rivers of Australia and the Nile. They are known as lung-fishes and are able to survive buried in mud where later developments of gill-breathers would certainly die. There is no suggestion that their survival was the result of trial and error, or rivalry with their neighbours, for they appear to be members of the earliest known class of true fishes to be produced. They were a success from the start, have seen the dinosaurs come and go and have had their pictures painted on the walls of ancient Egypt. What they feed on I don't know; but one suspects that their food may be minute organisms on the river floors. They are certainly not active hunters.

Amongst the innumerable types of gill-breathing, bony fishes which occupy the upper levels of the sea, there is of course an unending reign of murder. Kill or be killed is the rule, although, as far as I know, there is no evidence that any particular species fails to survive, even if man catches it in vast quantities. Cod once became scarce in the Channel approaches; but they are coming back again. A cod does not, at first glance, appear to be as efficiently designed as, say, a mackerel. It has no scale armour such as must, to some extent, protect the herring. It has something resembling an asdic device under its chin, which perhaps adds considerably to its efficiency. But the real reason the cod does so well must surely be that it produces such a vast quantity of eggs. Specimens have been measured in which the roe is half the weight of the whole fish and estimates have suggested that a single cod may lay seven million eggs. It is voracious and does not seem to care much what it eats, ranging from dog-fish to various kinds of crabs and lobsters. Like the salmon, after spawning the cod is in such poor condition that it takes a long time to recover. I caught a great cod once on a hand line, which was so weak it could hardly flap its tail. For an appreciable part of its life it is a lank miserable thing. It is not especially agile and it is not a fast streamlined beauty full of dash and energy like the mackerel. It survives, in fact, simply because it lays a lot of eggs. The same is apparently true of the herring. Everything is after it from the grey seal off the skerry to the gannet plunging down out of the clear blue sky. For a thousand years man has netted it by the million. Yet back the shoals come in apparently little diminished numbers. It cannot be a great murderer itself and presumably much of its diet is plankton. Yet it too, like the cod, has a relatively enormous roe.

So apparently these two fish, whose food value to mankind is enormous, do not owe their success to their superiority in warfare over their neighbours, but simply to their fecundity. How this could have been increased by trial and error, racial telepathy, or any other stimulation of the genes, is hard to imagine.

It would become boring if I wrote much more about these fish. I will not even speculate as to why deep-sea fish are lit up like cruising liners, which would, one imagines, give away their positions at once to their foes. But there is another point of general interest and importance.

The current belief is that the reign of terror in the seas forced animals out of them to colonize the land. Is there any truth in this? Since the theory is taught everywhere to children as a fact, it would be just as well if it were true; but is it? Can we see anywhere in the world today cases of animals flying from their enemies in the sea and taking refuge on the land? I cannot think of any and if I had ever heard of one I feel sure I would have remembered it. But there are cases, all over the world, of fish which do crawl out of the water and stay out for a time.

There is one little fish, very common on our own shores, which does this. Anyone who has pottered about the pools on a rocky beach must have heard it, even if they have not seen it. It is the common blenny, or shanny, *Blennius pholis*, (fig. 3.2). There is something mysterious about this little fish, for although you may often find and see him in a rock pool and you frequently hear him plopping into one, it is nearly impossible to catch sight of him while he is ashore. He seems to know that you are coming while you are still out of sight. But he has been observed to wriggle up on to a rock by using the shoulder muscles of his fins. It is like the fabulous booberie of the Scottish Highlands, which makes a splash behind you when you are fishing for trout from a boat in a hill loch. When you hear that splash it is time to go home, for 'the booberie is a bad beast'. In the same way there is something rather creepy about the splash of the shanny you have not seen. You always hear it when everything is fine and calm and usually behind your back. It sounds a much bigger splash than ought to be made by a little fellow no bigger than a large sardine out of a tin. But why does he climb up on to a rock at all?

Now if you search the pools in which shannies live with a shrimping net, you can get a very fair idea what is in them. You may catch a few shrimps, a crab or two, or an occasional little octopus. But you are most unlikely to find anything which might frighten him into leaving the water. It seems that he climbs out for no other reason than to sit in the sun and enjoy himself. As far as I can learn the same is true for all the other climbing fish. They climb up out of peaceful waters on to beaches, rocks or tree stumps and sit there appreciating the novel view. Nature: red in tooth and claw, indeed! This is more like the Liverpudlian going to the Lake District.

But I never said that evolution did not take place. I only said that the Darwinian theory was only a half-truth and therefore probably no truth at all. I think that the shanny can tell us something of the whole truth; but it may take till the end of this book to give a reasonable idea of what that is.

Now the geological record, compiled from the fossils collected over a long period of years by numerous enthusiasts, apparently tells us that the earliest land-animals were amphibians, at home both on land and in the water, frogs, newts, toads, turtles and such-like beasts. We see no turtles here save for a few washed up on our west coasts, which have been carried across the Atlantic by south-west gales and the North Atlantic Drift. But we all know frogs, newts and toads. The life history of the frog is taught to everybody and many children keep tadpoles and can watch the whole development for themselves. But although it

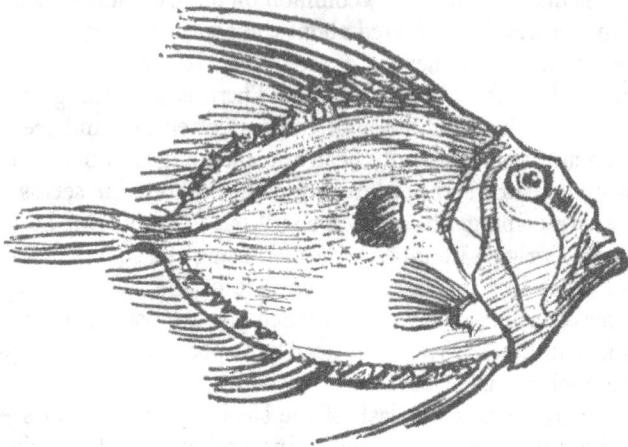

1

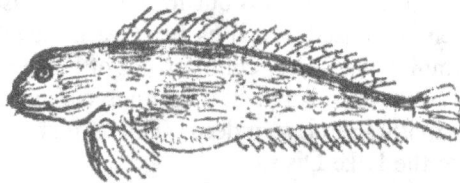

2

Figure 3 Two fishes mentioned in the text. 1. The John Dory. Small specimen, 6″ long. 2. The Shanny. Specimen, 5″ long.

seems reasonably certain that amphibians must have come from bony fishes in some way, there is no visual evidence for it in the rocks. In fact it has been frequently noticed that all the great families in nature seem to start already developed as birds, or mammals, or reptiles and so on. At the point in time at which they seem to have appeared there is a blank in the record. The blenny family does, however, give us a good clue to what seems to have happened. The blennies seem to be explorers. They climb up a rock, or a tree root or shamble up a beach because they like it. From some ancestral forms of blenny then we might expect the colonization of the land to have begun. At one stage of its embryo life the young frog or newt is very much like an embryo fish. In fact there is something about our shanny's head which makes us think of frogs and newts.

Very well then, we will take as a starting point that blennoid fish somehow evolved into amphibians and see what happens. It already seems improbable that their evolution was forced on them by a need to escape the ravenous attentions of their neighbours in the seas. They came ashore to please themselves. But a very great difficulty now appears. When the amphibians start to be found as fossils they are complete amphibians. They have four jointed legs with digits on them.

Everyone today is brought up on the theory that all characteristics are carried by the genes, and mutations can occur by a change in the order of the chromosomes. This theory is probably quite reliable as far as it goes. But does anyone seriously envisage a jointed leg with toes on it being slowly evolved in this manner? One can perhaps imagine that the effort of wriggling up the beach tended to produce a change in shape of the fishes' front, the pectoral fins. But we are also told by Darwinian evolutionists that acquired characteristics cannot be transmitted to the offspring of the animals which acquire them. We will assume that this is wrong and that the blennoid fish slowly developed longer ones for their front fins, that some of the rays in the fins themselves joined together and produced a second bony extension of the first and that somehow digits evolved together with wrist bones to enable them to move about. Thus you have the framework of a leg. Of course all the muscles, nerves, blood vessels and so on have also to be modified and extended; but what of that? It is unfortunate that there are no fossils available to show this process taking place, but it may have happened. Actually the development of the tadpole shows what must really have taken place. The hind legs develop first and then the front legs grow. But a fish is not built in such a way that this could happen in adult life. All land vertebrates from frog to man and including birds have to have a strong bony structure attached to the back-bone on which the hinder pair of legs or, in the case of birds, the only pair of legs hinge. But with almost all fish there is no lateral pair of fins except in front of the body. So, although there is something in the nature of a cartilagenous arch which might conceivably have mutated into a pelvic girdle, there are no paired fins which could have developed into hind legs. Since the hind legs are of much greater importance than front ones, for they have to carry most of an animal's weight, it seems evident that the change from fish to amphibian cannot have taken place by mutations in the structure of the adults. Here we have a race of fish which is well on the way to becoming amphibian in habits, but it seems quite impossible that they could have become amphibian in structure. It seems far more reasonable to suppose that the idea of growing legs was thought out in detail by some external mind and then added to the embryo state.

So far in this study we have found little to support the Darwinian Theory of Evolution. The complexity of the design of the sailing jelly-fish, *Velella*, seems quite beyond the possibility of any chance development. When we find a family of fish which appears to be well on the way to leaving the water for the land, we see that, far from being driven by fiercer rivals to do so, they do it simply because they enjoy sitting in the sun. The most powerful fish in northern waters turns out to be a semi-vegetarian living on plankton, while two of the most important food-fishes owe their great numbers to the multitude of their eggs. Competition is far fiercer in the water than on land, yet many primitive forms survive without difficulty for millions of years. It seems probable then that the great variety of form, and above all the beauty of colour, of fishes has nothing to do with competition and must be ascribed to an entirely different cause.

It is usual for those who think about the great variety-show of nature to visualize it as an orderly succession of development starting with the formless amoeba and ending up with man. A family tree is drawn up which shows where each great branch, known as a phylum, left the parent stem and spread out on its own evolving course. This looks tidy and convincing, even though like many another family tree it has many gaps and guesses in it. It used to be, and still is, widely believed, that if you reduced living tissue to its smallest components you would eventually discover what life is and so be able to produce living organisms. But even if this should in the end prove true and the germ of life be found, there is still another factor. You cannot make that germ of life develop without adding thought to it. Life must always be a compound of its chemical constituents and mind itself. And you cannot take mind to pieces and examine it under a microscope. When

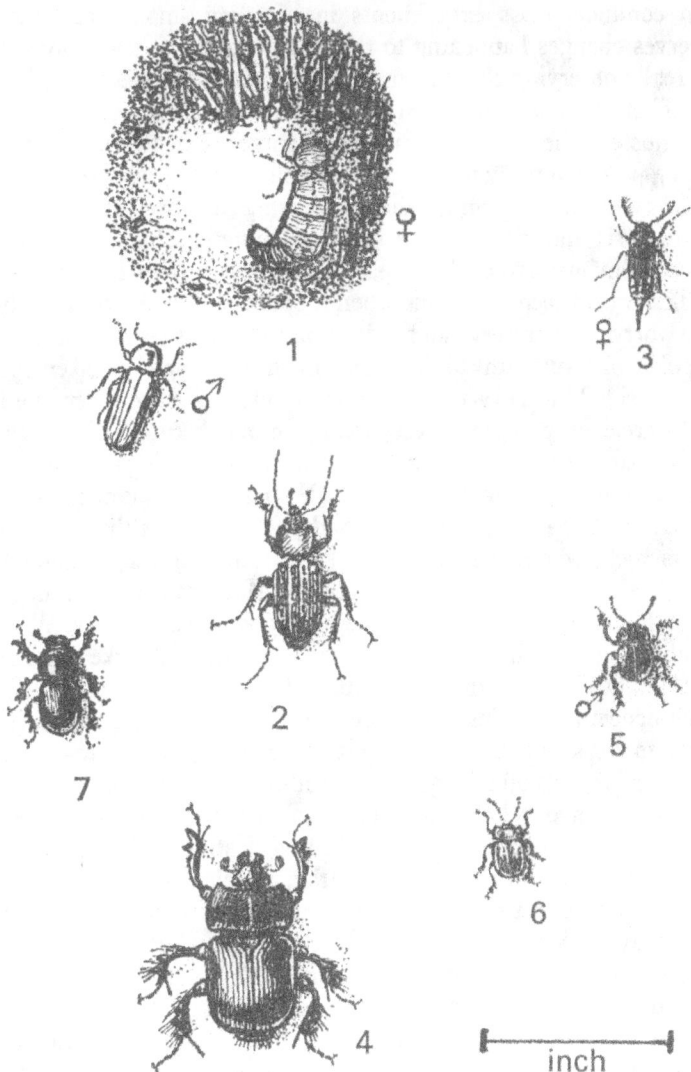

Figure 4 Various beetles mentioned in the text. 1. Glow-worm, *Lampyris noctiluca* (brown). 2. *Carabus arvensis* (copper). 3. *Metoecus paradoxus* (yellow-black). 4. *Geotrupes stercorarius* (steel blue). 5. *Chrysomela goetingensis* (shining violet). 6. *Chrysomela fastuosa* (blue and gold stripes on brilliant emerald). 7. *Aphodius ater* (black).

man conducts mass experiments in breeding small organisms and observes changes happening to them after so many generations, he is not really observing changes in natural genetics, but these changes plus the effect of his own mind on the organism. I hope to show later that this must be the case. You cannot do anything in this world without adding part of your own mind to what you do. It is probably man's own restless and unhappy mind which is causing the observed variations in the bacteria and viruses from which he suffers. This is why he only succeeds in mastering one disease for a new variety to appear. The medical world recognizes this when it speaks of psychosomatic illness. The worry, fuss, misery and tiredness in the man is transferred by what is spoken of as telepathy to the micro-organisms which had taken up residence inside him. He is upset, so they are upset and then they bite him.

This telepathy functions very weakly in man because it is smothered by too many other happenings; but it is still in working order and most of us communicate by it at times. In the rest of the animal world it is far stronger. It is presumably telepathy which makes the shanny dive off its rock, where it was happily sunbathing until some thought of yours was picked up by its radar screen. Much might be learnt about telepathy by an investigation of the blenny family as a whole. Why, for instance, are so many species fitted with curious antler-like appendages on their heads? Are these telepathic 'scanners'? We know that the tassel beneath the chins of the cod family has a strong nerve in it and seems to work as a kind of asdic. It seems very probable that a somewhat similar unusual fitting, on the heads of a semi-amphibious race of fish, has been developed to protect them with radar when they go ashore. Much that is glibly described as 'instinct' when observed in animals is in fact reaction to telepathy, which is so little studied by most zoologists that they hardly recognize the existence of that faculty. They have a long way to go before they can become qualified to manufacture or modify living organisms.

I am not unusual in looking for signs of telepathy in nature. In 1947 Professor A. C. Hardy, when President of the Zoological section of the British Association's Newcastle Meeting, made a devastating denunciation of the mechanistic biologists, whose 'dogmatic assertions put forward as if they had the authority of true science must, I think, be extremely damaging to civilization'. He went on to suggest that something akin to telepathy might be 'found to be a factor in moulding the patterns of behaviour among members of a species', and suggested that this might change the outlook on evolution. Well indeed it might. That theory is a pyramid of supposition balanced on an apex of conjecture and is already viewed with suspicion by many able physicists.

Three

If we want to see the Darwinian Theory of Evolution at its most unsatisfactory point, we should take a short look at the insects. To begin with, how does an insect evolve at all? It is a most complicated mechanism to have been derived from what some evolutionists call a 'piece of animate jelly'. I suppose we are expected to visualize numerous pieces of jelly warring with and eating each other until some are stimulated to produce bigger and better jellies and so on. Really this seems an incredibly stupid theory and it is no wonder that Adam Sedgwick found parts of Darwin's thesis ludicrous, with the rest tending to degrade humanity. Darwin himself seems to have been persuaded that there was something wrong with it and in his last edition of the *Origin of Species*, more or less admitted it. But Thomas Huxley and the philosopher Spencer, who had jumped on the evolutionary band-wagon, were made of sterner stuff. Their fervid propaganda coupled with the clumsiness of the opposition won a surprising and rapid victory. But they never convinced everybody and their successes were to a large extent, and to this day remain, more or less confined to Britain, America and Russia. France, who for generations had produced great naturalists, would have nothing to do with it and still proclaims that it does not work.

But supposing, for a moment, we admit that the struggle for existence and the survival of the fittest might, after millions of years, produce a segmented animal with jointed legs from a lump of living jelly, how are we to explain the three complete changes which then take place in its life cycle? If we include the egg, there are four changes. The egg hatches into the larva, which appears to be a complete animal in itself. This larva spends what looks like a lifetime feeding on this or that. Then the larva dies outwardly and grows a new form of outer covering for a period of rest or sleep as a pupa. Lastly the outer covering dies again and from it emerges the perfect insect, the imago, which looks so different from the larval stage that it is hard to believe the two phases belong to a single individual. Only the imago can breed, and starts the cycle off again by laying eggs. All this remarkable performance is assumed by the Darwinist to have been evolved by a long series of slow mutations, which gave some advantage to the original lump of jelly. If you had never heard of the Theory of Evolution, nor been taught to accept it as having been proved, would you not think that the whole idea was complete and utter rubbish? But the sequence of events is fact. A lump of living jelly is at the root of all living things. The insect does develop through its three metamorphoses. The perfect insects were produced so long ago that no one knows how it happened; but species of dragon-flies, nearly two foot wide across the wings, were flying about over the swamps in which our coal seams were formed. In these carboniferous beds the largest known animals were early amphibians, about which we have already talked. From a lump of jelly a fish ancestor was somehow produced. From a lump of jelly an insect ancestor was evolved. From the fish ancestor somehow there developed an amphibian ancestor. But it is completely inconceivable that any of this came about through the pressures imagined by the Darwinists. Some far more powerful factor has been left out of their calculations. That factor must be mental, and the means by which its thoughts are applied, telepathic.

I have had an interest in insects since I was a boy at school. Their great variety and frequent beauty fascinates and also intrigues. Why are there so many varieties and what has given them attractive shapes and colours for what purpose? I was not greatly interested in moths and butterflies. So many people collected and studied these that there was little scope for finding anything new. But there were more than three thousand species of British beetles and few people collected these. Dragon-flies too seemed to be little studied, although few insects are more beautiful. Finally there are the wasps and bees, especially the 'solitary' ones, whose life stories are frequently most unexpected.

It is from these groups, about which I have some knowledge from personal observation, that I am going to take a few examples and to discuss them from the point of view of evolution. I do not like to take too many or treat them in too much detail, for it is so easy to become a bore. For the same reason I always try to keep technical terms to a minimum. It is all too easy to give a specious impression of deep learning by flooding a page with technical jargon; I avoid it when I can and do not use footnotes. I remember once reading what would have been an interesting article on some Scottish battle, if it had been confined to a brief statement of observed fact. Instead it contained about two dozen reference numbers. Having looked them up I found that in almost every case they referred back to a couple of entries in old chronicles. Vast study was suggested where little had really been done.

Everyone interested in the subject knew the entries in any case. Occasionally one has to use them when one forgets something of importance, not remembering it till everything has been tidily typed out. Then one must put in a footnote or refer to some note at the end of the chapter.

Now I will talk a little about insects providing food for their unborn offspring. I suppose you could say that such species as do this are fitter to survive than those which do not. However there is such clear evidence that great thought and discrimination has somehow been exercised in the choice of food and also in its preservation, that the survival equation is relatively unimportant. A simple example of food storage is found in the common genus of *Geotrupes*, which most people familiar with the country must know well (fig. 4.4). There are six British species and they are related to the almost fabulous scarabs of the East. *Geotrupes* flies to dung. (In these days, when horses have become scarce, this generally means that it goes to a cow-pat.) The fertilized female beetle burrows into the dung and then down into the soil below it. There it sinks a vertical tunnel a foot or so deep. The end of the tunnel is then used as a store-chamber for a quantity of dung considerably larger in volume than the beetle itself. In these store-chambers the eggs are laid. The larvae hatch out, feed on the dung, grow to full size (approximately the same as the parent), turn into pupae and after a period of quiescence eventually appear again on the surface as perfect insects. This cycle is, of course, much the same as that of blow flies in meat and very many other forms. The difference, however, lies in the construction of the store-chamber and stocking it with food for larvae as yet unborn. This is clear evidence of thought on somebody's part, whether by the beetle itself or by some external agency; thought postulates a mind. It will be part of our argument later on to show how the beetle finds some dung at all and does not spend its life till it is worn out, aimlessly wandering through a forest of grass. It does not do this. It flies direct to the dung and many people must have heard *Geotrupes* droning overhead on a summer evening, a sound which has earned it the country name of 'Dumble dor.'

Now the *Geotrupes* family all sink these tunnels, and store food for their young whom they never see or apparently know about. But there is a closely allied genus called *Aphodius*, which does not do this. There are more than thirty British species (fig. 4.7). They are far more numerous than *Geotrupes*. Cow-pats are usually full of them, with two or three species in each pat. *Aphodius* is much smaller than *Geotrupes*. They do not store food and are much more vulnerable to crows, rooks and magpies. The whole life cycle of *Aphodius* takes place in the pat itself. They mate inside it and lay their eggs. The eggs hatch, the larvae emerge and feed on the drying dung around them. They then pupate on the surface of the ground and, if lucky, hatch out into a perfect insect. It may be of general interest to remark that the first hoopoe I saw in England was happily digging for beetles in a cow-pat on the green lane known as Worstead Street near Cambridge.

Now there is no struggle for existence in a cow-pat as such. The beetles which live on it are vegetarian and there is plenty of food for all who come. Yet there are two very similar families, *Geotrupes* and *Aphodius*. *Geotrupes* lays its eggs deep underground, where they hatch and the larvae grow up in perfect safety, except perhaps for the chance appearance of a mole. *Aphodius* leaves its young quite unprotected on the surface of the ground, where they must be eaten in thousands by birds. Both genera are attacked by mites, but, though doubtless most uncomfortable, this is not fatal. If there was any truth in the Darwinian hypothesis, the genus *Aphodius* ought to have been more or less exterminated and the ingenious *Geotrupes* to have flourished exceedingly. Yet this is not the case; *Aphodius* is infinitely more numerous.

Now let us look for a moment at a more complicated type of food-storing. I will make it general and not bother the reader with the difficult names of species. There are numerous kinds of solitary wasp and all their life cycles are different. The best place to learn something about them is on a sandy heath where there are patches more or less bare of vegetation. On a hot summer day you will often find numbers of small, round holes in these patches looking, sometimes, rather like the mark made by a bullet shot from a ·22 rifle into a board, but often surrounded by a little cone of sand. If you approach these holes very carefully you will now and then surprise the eyes and antennae of a small wasp peering out of the top. Elsewhere you may find fine sandy soil being tipped out of another hole. If one of these holes is excavated with great care, digging it transversely and leaving a vertical face, it will be seen that it leads into a sloping tunnel perhaps a foot in length. This has frequently been done and the almost incredible story I am telling is observed fact. Somewhere along the tunnel, not always at the end, a small chamber has been excavated by the mother wasp. Apparently the father is unmoved by her exertions and goes away to amuse and feed himself. In the chamber are several little hunting-spiders, each with a wasp's egg on it. They are not dead, but are paralysed.

What happens is this. Each species of wasp preys on a particular species of hunting-spider. Occasionally it makes a mistake and secures a similar type; but in general you can say that one kind of wasp only feeds on one kind of spider. Hunting-spiders, often smartly barred in black and white, are the little webless kinds you see darting about almost anywhere. These sand wasps are very fast and agile. It does not usually take them long to capture a spider. This it stings in exactly the right spot to paralyse and not kill it. It then carries the spider to the hole, drags it down, puts it in the prepared chamber and lays an egg on it. Then it goes off to fetch another spider, and repeats the process till the chamber is full. The tunnel is finally blocked and the eggs left to hatch on the spiders. When the wasp larva hatches from the egg, it finds its necessary food alive and ready to eat. Ruthless this may seem to us, but it is obvious that it has all been thought out with extreme care. Clearly it is not all thought out afresh each time a wasp is fertilized. It is a mental process made available telepathically to each female wasp in its turn. It cannot be a group thought-process in our ordinary time sequence; but something on what appears to be another plane of existence where time does not occur as we know it. It seems most unlikely that wasps ever thought it up for themselves. Even if you can imagine a process by which a sand wasp was evolved by natural selection, it is surely impossible to extend such reasoning to include the remarkable manner in which such a wasp afterwards behaved. How, for instance, did it learn the exact spot in which to sting the spider so that it remained paralysed (fig. 5.3) but alive? And where does the struggle for existence come in? I cannot think of any-thing likely to prey on the wasps, unless perhaps a stray wheatear might do so. The nightjar, which is a great insect-eater and found nesting on sandy heaths, only does its hunting at night. Bats are ruled out for the same reason. We will leave the sand wasps for a while, dashing in and out among the heather or peeping out of the top of their burrows, and go back to take a short look at some other members of the beetle family.

Perhaps one of the most remarkable developments of land animals is the light of the female glow-worm. The male insect is a very ordinary looking beetle (fig. 4.1). But the female is a most inefficient looking specimen. It has no wings, whereas the male can fly strongly. The abdomen, as it is called of all beetles, is jointed and the last two seg-ments of this female glow-worm give out a brilliant, pale greenish light, which I have seen over fifty yards away in the darkness of a summer night. The light can be turned on or off. When the female wishes to attract the male she turns it on and he flies to the light and joins her. That is all there is to it. But how did it come about? The Darwinists would have to say that some mutation of the genes caused a minute change in the lower abdominal segments of a female and caused these to give off a little light. This was so successful that such female beetles as were provided with this light secured more mates than those that did not and so through many generations the lightless females were un-mated and that form died out. Only the ones with lights succeeded and the lights grew brighter and brighter. That does not of course tell us how the first lights originated. As a matter of fact there is a faint glow from the bottom segments of the male. Both male and female were provided with a rudimentary light. In fact it seems probable that at one time both sexes flew and the process we are looking at is one of de-volution. There was no need for the female to fly, and by degrees the wings and wing-cases atrophied, became rudimentary and finally vanished. There are plenty of cases in nature of this process of de-volution. In fact, if the world goes on as it is going at present, humanity, starting with the Americans, will probably lose the use of its legs. Of course our little glow-worms are just tame relations of the brilliant fire-flies of the tropics and there both sexes light up brightly. We are no further forward in learning how the lights originated; but it seems to have nothing to do with the natural selection of the brighter females. One might almost think that the lights, like those on deep-sea fish, were put there for the enjoyment of some external mind and came into existence with no evolution at all.

Then there is the puzzle of the beetles which are found living in the nests of ants and wasps. They are found nowhere else and a single species of beetle is apparently attached to only one kind of ant. Of course ants have a passion for substances which are sweet and sticky. They milk and foster aphids, putting them where they want them and treating them like cows. They are known to take the larvae of the Large Blue butterfly into their nests and feed them on their own spare larvae for the same reason. But it is not known whether the parasitic beetles exude something delectable. Whatever the reason, the beetles appar-ently spend all their lives and go through all their changes in the ants' nests without being molested. They are dull little things with no wings. It is very hard to see how they could have become widely distributed and relatively common by any struggle on their own part. The ants again seem to be responsible for their distribution.

As far as one knows wasps do not share the ants' passion for sweet and sticky juices from other insects, but there is a parasitic beetle, *Metoecus paradoxus* (fig. 4.3) in the nests of the common wasp. The only wasp's nest I have taken to see if I could find the beetle, had several specimens in it. But people are nervous of wasps and the life story of the parasite does not appear to be known. It has wing-cases, but I very much doubt whether it ever flies.

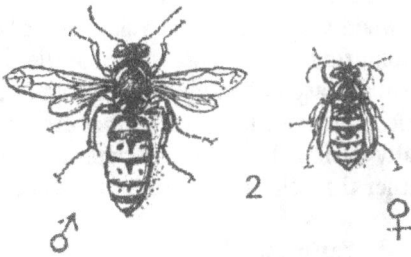

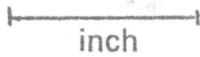

Figure 5 Yellow for Danger. 1. Hornet, *Vespa crabro*, yellow with chestnut thorax and bands. These are workers. 2. Common wasp, *Vespa vulgaris*, drone and worker, yellow and black. 3. Solitary wasp, black and yellow. A spider hunter.

33

It would be interesting to know whether there is a similar but larger beetle in the nest of the hornet. But to find out one would have to destroy the nests. I should be sorry to do that. I rather like the ponderous old monsters. There are plenty here at Hole and a few days ago two came together into the room where I was writing this (fig. 5.1). I hoped they would not settle on me as that would have entailed some strength of mind not to brush them away in alarm. However, after carefully examining the room for spiders, they flew out again and went on hunting the undersides of the rain-water guttering. I have seen a hornet's nest which had been destroyed in a hollow tree. The cells of the honeycomb are enormous.

Of course it would be possible to say that these parasitic beetles had been driven into the nests of their hosts to seek protection from their enemies outside. In that case, however, surely many other insects would do the same and you would find a varied host of beetles inside. What you do find is a family of beetles carefully graded to fit the size of their hosts. A species in the nest of a small ant is roughly the size of that ant. In the nest of the large wood ant the beetle is relatively larger: it also approximates to the colouring of its host. The beetle in the wasp's nests is the size of a small wasp and coloured black and yellow. There are no ant's nest beetles in the wasp's nest. In fact each species appears to have been specially designed to accommodate with its host and this implies thought, rather than chance mutation, on somebody's part.

Insects are essentially land creatures. There is only one species known which belongs entirely to the sea and that is in the Pacific Ocean. Many of them make use of, and even spend all their lives in, fresh water, but there is no evidence whatsoever that the order of insects was once driven to colonize the land by pressures in the sea. It just does not seem to have happened that way. Had the ancient seas been swarming with insects it is inconceivable that their fossils should not have been found frequently. The hard chitin with which they are covered is very resistant to decay. I once excavated the remains of a flea from an Anglo-Saxon grave! It had been at least thirteen hundred years in the ground and was still perfectly recognizable. Archaeologists do not find such things nowadays. The mathematical precision of the holes they dig has become far more important than what comes out of them. Vital and often quite large objects are left behind in the spoil. Exact measurement was not used in antiquity. An inch or two error in an excavated plan means nothing at all. But the finding and observation of the location of objects in relation to levels and so on is vital. What is the value of the excavation of a whole wheel-house in the Hebrides

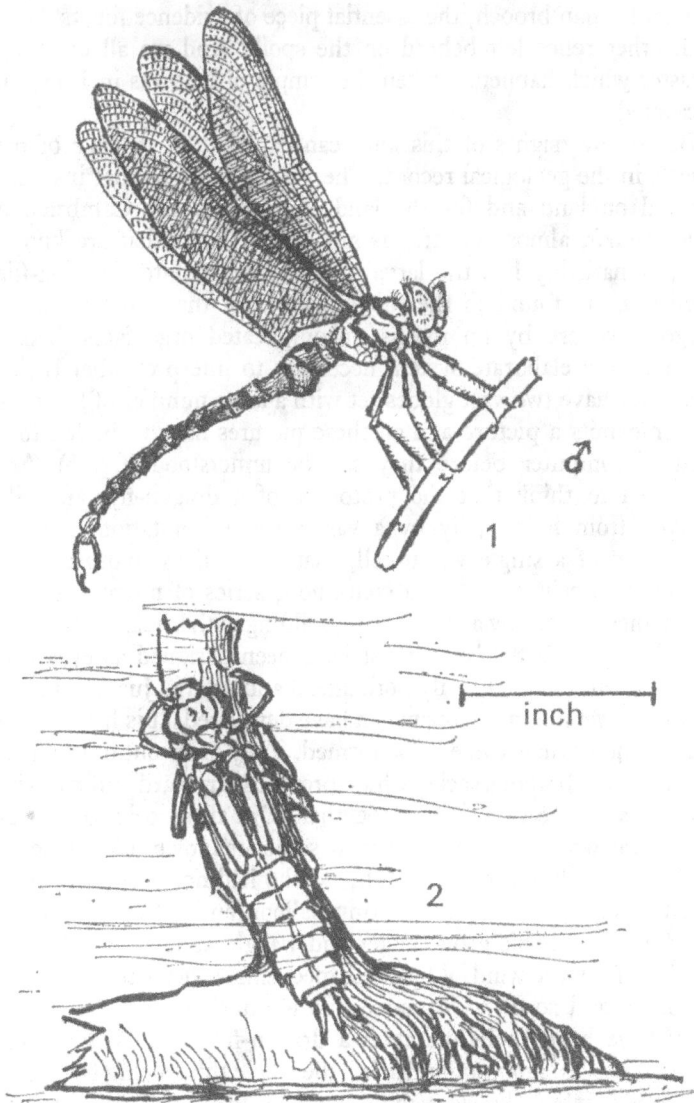

Figure 6 Dragon-fly imago and nymph. 1. *Æschna cyanea* (yellow head and thorax with brown streaks; body, blue, green and brown). 2. Nymph on water-logged stick. Although this fine insect is 2¾″ long, it is less than a fifth the size of dragon-flies of the Carboniferous.

when a Roman brooch, the essential piece of evidence for its dating, is with other relics left behind on the spoil? And we all know of the disaster which happened when the temple of Mithras in London was excavated.

But no oversights of this kind can explain the absence of marine insects in the geological record. The answer must be that insects were evolved on land and for the land. A fossil in the Cambrian beds, *Hymenocaris*, almost as early as any living things that are known of, looks remarkably like the larva of a giant mosquito. Dragon-flies of giant size are found in the fossil swamps of the coal-measures. But dragon-flies are by no means uncomplicated organisms. Take, for instance, the elaborate system necessary to interpret what their eyes see. They have two vast globes set with a large number of lenses. Each lens transmits a picture and all these pictures have to be fed to some kind of computer before they can be understood (fig. 6). Are we supposed to think that the prototype of a dragon-fly, after it had evolved from living jelly by a vast series of mutations, came into possession of a single visual cell, that this cell by another mutation became two cells and then a continuous series of mutations built up two domes of sight by a process like building with bricks? This is senseless. The dragon-fly's eyes must have been designed as eyes suitable for a creature which can fly both ahead and astern. Just try to picture how the reversing mechanism can have developed. It is hard enough to imagine how wings came to be formed. They grow out of the insect as a pair of membranous sacks, which presently dry hard and flat with the two sides of the sack joined together. Did these originate as single cells from which the insect gained some unknown advantage which made it more fitted to survive others who had not produced this cell? Did this cell then evolve as a tiny balloon and act as a rudimentary parachute? Did this grow longer and waggle about so that the insect was blown by the wind? Did some mechanism then cause the balloons to rotate, and so on? Of course this is utterly absurd. A dragon-fly must have been thought out as a dragon-fly down to the minutest detail of nerves, limbs and muscles, the whole thing being formed out of living cells which knew exactly where to grow and when to divide. There must have been a complete series of blue-prints like a cinema film before the perfect insect could grow at all. And this is not all.

There must have been another series of blue-prints before the egg developed into a repulsive-looking crocodilian larva known as a nymph, which grew under water and murdered other creatures, with a mouth like an extensible grab. This, after an apparent lifetime in the water, has to climb out, turn into a chrysalis by another elaborate series of cell changes and at last emerge as the perfect flying insect. I simply cannot see any of the catch-phrases of the Darwinian evolutionist having anything to do with a dragon-fly. It is far less absurd and improbable to imagine that the whole process was deliberately thought out by some powerful mentality quite external to the dragon-fly itself. I am not alone in thinking in this way. Physiologists have been realizing in recent years how difficult it is to account for the way in which a human embryo develops without assuming the existence of some kind of blue-print. You cannot have blue-prints and Natural Selection at the same time. One or the other, or both ideas must be wrong.

Four

To many people the most spectacular phase of geological time is the age which was filled with great lizards, the Dinosaurs (a name meaning 'terrible lizards'). For millions of years the fossils tell a story of an earth covered with monsters, walking, running, jumping, swimming and flying. They reached a bulk never attained before or since, except perhaps by the fin whales, and lengths of over eighty feet. They dwarfed the large amphibians who went before them, and appeared to be the end-product of evolution. Then, for some unknown reason, they almost all died out. There are dinosaurs, of course, still with us today; crocodiles and alligators are the largest examples. But the age of the great lizards ended, as it had begun, in mystery. How lizards evolved no one knows. In one age there are no lizards, and in the next the world is full of them. It is the same story with every great natural order; no one can do more than guess how it came into being. There are no carefully graded successions of missing-link fossils. We know that there are enormous gaps in the record, but all the same that record is very extensive. It is surely big enough to show one order leading on to the next if this had really happened. It never does. We tried it out with the blennies and the amphibians and were met with failure. We cannot understand how the orders evolved by making use of the Darwinian theory; but we can understand if we make use of another. Looking backwards over the whole geological picture, it all makes sense if we assume that some mind, not differing much from a human mind except in degree, was experimenting with living things. Leave out the word 'chance' and substitute 'intention' and everything becomes reasonable. This is still the belief of millions today and always was so. Before we go into this problem further, however, it seems to be important to see whether the evidence from the study of botany has anything to tell us.

England is a land of deciduous trees, which means that their leaves fall off in winter and grow again in the following spring. Each year also, they go through a cycle of producing first flowers, and when these are fertilized, they fruit. To most casual observers many of these trees look much alike and one has to learn the differences between oak, walnut, ash, chestnut, beech, elm, lime or poplar. However, when one comes to look at their fruits, each tree produces some design entirely different from the next. The oak, for instance, yields a large, shiny, brown bullet, whereas the sycamore, which is not so very different to look at, has a remarkable device like a double-bladed propeller to carry two seeds away on the wind. The walnut has a double-shelled nut enclosed in a fleshy case, beloved by rooks, and the Spanish chestnut a prickly husk apparently designed to catch on the fur of large animals. However different these fruits may be, the seed itself develops on germination in much the same way. A single shoot emerges from it, which divides into two branches. One goes down into the earth and becomes the root; the other goes up into the air and soon produces a pair of leaves (fig. 7.1). Before many weeks have passed a complete baby tree is growing on the spot where the seed ultimately came to rest. Therefore it is clear that all the properties of the original tree are in the seed, and must have been there soon after it was fertilized. The tree has no say in its evolution. If there is any evolution it is in the seed. In fact this appears to be true of all animal and vegetable life. The changes which lead to variation are not those of the adult animals, but something which happens to the unborn children. Darwin's postulated elongation of the giraffe's neck could never have taken place in its adult life. It could only have taken place, if indeed it did develop at all, by the adult giraffe thinking: 'By Jove! it would be nice if I had a longer neck and could reach those leaves at the tops of the trees.' This thought would then have to have taken effect on the genes of its unborn children. The message might be supposed to reach those genes telepathically so that they altered the arrangement of their chromosomes to produce mutations with long necks. Well and good. This is a possibility of course. But consider trees. Each tree would have to send thoughts to its seeds something like this: 'I say, boys, you've got to grow now so that you will have a prickly case. Then this will hang up in the wool of sheep and be carried away somewhere else so that you can succeed in the struggle for existence.' But where is the struggle for existence in the case of full grown trees? There isn't one. It all took place many years before, when the tree was only a seedling and had perhaps to fight its way upward through grass, or fern, or bramble. Each type of tree too would have to have been capable of intense and exact thought in order to produce seeds to a specific pattern. What could be more different than the acorn, the sycamore seed and that of the Spanish chestnut? Can anyone really believe that all these different ways of seed distribution were the result of chance

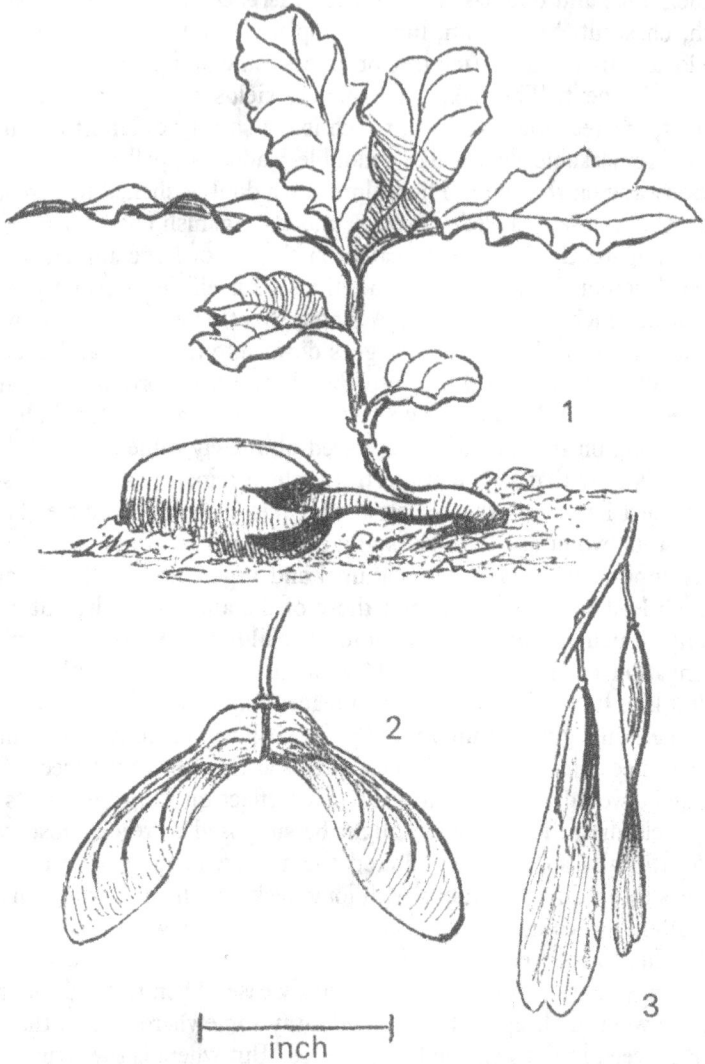

Figure 7 Seeds of trees. 1. Oak seedling germinated from an acorn. 2. Winged sycamore seeds which rotate when falling. 3. Ash seeds, deliberately formed with a twist to cause rotation.

mutation? As a Hungarian friend used to say to me: 'Tom, it is a nonsense.'

Then we see another remarkable thing. Other plants of quite different families have very similar forms of seed distribution. There is the elaborate parachute device of thistles and dandelions to make use of the wind. There is the prickle-covered seed-container of the burdock, agrimony, houndstongue, goosegrass or barley, or the long protein containers of beans and peas, comparable to the acorn and developing in exactly the same way. Isn't it obvious that these seed-containing devices were thought out independently of the actual designs of the plants themselves and then added to these plants? Just as the walnut was intended to be carried away and its outside eaten by rooks, leaving the hard shell to develop in some place far from the parent tree, so were the soft fruits of strawberry, currant or yew. The seeds were meant to pass right through the birds, which ate the berries, and to be dropped somewhere else. The mistletoe is an outstanding example, for this plant has to grow in the crevices of the bark of trees. The white berry is so sticky that when birds eat them they have to wipe their beaks hard on the branches and so push the seeds into cracks.

One could continue writing about such things. Every case would indicate thought and careful planning, the exact opposite of casual chance evolution. There is no place for this in the botanical world.

Take, for instance, the carnivorous plants. These are only represented here by small and inconspicuous examples, butterworts and sundews (fig. 8). But in warmer climates you find startling examples, such as the well-known Pitcher plants and Venus' Fly-Traps. I used to grow sundews as a boy. They are common on the wet parts of heathery moors. The upper sides of their leaves are covered with hairs, which exude globules of sticky liquid at their tips. When a small insect touches one of these globules, not only does it stick there, but all the neighbouring hairs bend over towards the victim and it is held like a fly in a spider's web. Then the plant slowly absorbs the victim's juices. Here the Darwinist has to postulate several mutations beyond the development of a flowering plant itself. First there has to be the evolution of hairs, which are assumed to offer some advantage to the plant in its hypothetical struggle. Then some mutation has to result in the exudation of a sticky juice from the tips of the hairs presumably because the plant's metabolism was producing too much of this juice. Then yet another mutation had to cause great sensitivity on the part of the hairs and attraction towards anything touching a neighbour. Finally after assumed aeons of trial and error, the plant has to adapt itself to absorbing animal juices into its system. However long there

Figure 8 Two Ice Age survivals: one colonist and an insect eater. 1. *Pinguicula alpina* (white with yellow spots); very rare, if not extinct in Scotland. Norwegian specimen. 2. *Pinguicula lusitanica* (pink) colonizing? 3. *Pinguicula vulgaris* (violet). 4. Stunted form of *P. vulgaris* in Greenland. 5. *Drosera rotundifolia* (white insectivorous).

has been to complete this evolution, the chances against a perfect sundew being produced by its own efforts must run into many millions.

But there is a real 'struggle for existence' in the world of botany. It takes the form of one plant grabbing the soil on which another feeds. In this way the stronger grower smothers the weaker, and slowly displaces it. In this country you can watch the process taking place on an area of newly-disturbed ground, or on sand-dunes which are becoming anchored by grasses. The study of these processes, which is known as ecology, is one of the most interesting branches of botany, and appeals to me. I have long had a fancy for small alpine and arctic plants. In fact I have made paintings of most of the flowering plants of Jan Mayen and West Greenland in the intervals between archaeological and other activities and doubt whether there are any other such collections in existence.

The great interest in these small plants, excluding their attractive appearance, lies in their distribution. Some of them are found high up in the Swiss and Italian Alps, near shore-level in the Arctic, and isolated on the tops of high Scottish mountains. What happens in between these areas?

When I first began to take an interest in these 'alpines', in about 1920, the theory used to explain their sporadic distribution was that they were hardy plants, which had survived the last Ice Age. This idea, which was accepted for very many years, has been given up in favour of another. It is now thought that they represent the first wave of new plants coming in to colonize barren lands after the ice-sheets had melted (fig. 9). Either idea might be correct, or the answer might be a combination of the two. This is rather an interesting puzzle and it is perhaps worth spending a little time on it.

First then, geology recognizes a series of several waves of glaciation, the last of which was less intense in western Europe than the one which went before it. Between each glaciation there was what is known as an inter-glacial period, during which the ice-sheets either melted completely or became so small as to be negligible. The intervening inter-glacial periods may have been of the order of 20,000 years. If we are in one at the moment, as seems very likely, it is something like 10,000 years since the bulk of the country was covered with ice. We should be near the peak of an inter-glacial period.

But these glacial and inter-glacial periods do not seem to have taken place at the same time in different areas. The glaciations of the Alps and round about Switzerland do not quite coincide with British glaciations. So there would be periods during which cold-loving plants

Figure 9 Retreating or colonizing plants. 1. *Melandrium apetalum*. 2. *Phillodoce caerulea*. 3. *Rhododendron lapponicum*. 4. *Ledum palustre*. 5. *Mertensia maritima*. All from specimens which I drew in Greenland except 1 which is from Arctic Canada.

44

Figure 10 Maximum of an Ice Age. The Greenland Ice, several thousand feet thick, reaches Melville Bay. A little sparse vegetation grows near the shore on the islands.

would be growing in one area and not in the other. In the Arctic, of course, a glaciation is still going on, although it fluctuates considerably. Even during an intense Ice Age there are some areas which are ice-free in summer. Although the Greenland Ice Cap is several thousand feet thick in the middle, there are, here and there, rocky mountain-tops sticking out above it, while in places such as Melville Bay where the ice sheet comes down near the sea, there is still a fringe of off-shore islands where plants grow and where man has lived for five hundred years or more. I have not been on the Ice Cap and do not know whether anything grows on the mountain summits in the middle. But it is evident that if the Ice Cap were not so thick it would be possible to do so. The situation in the Highlands of Scotland was once very similar to that of Greenland today and scratches made by the ice have been observed very high up on the hill tops. It is probable, however, that these scratches cannot be dated with certainty to any particular glaciation. The last glaciation may well have left large enough mountain areas free from ice, on which inter-glacial plants could survive.

It was observed long ago that quite a large variety of alpine-arctic flowering plants (fig. 11.1, 2, 5) were to be found growing above 3,000 ft on certain Perthshire hills, in particular on Ben Lawers (3,984 ft). In fact, it came to be assumed that it was no use looking for

45

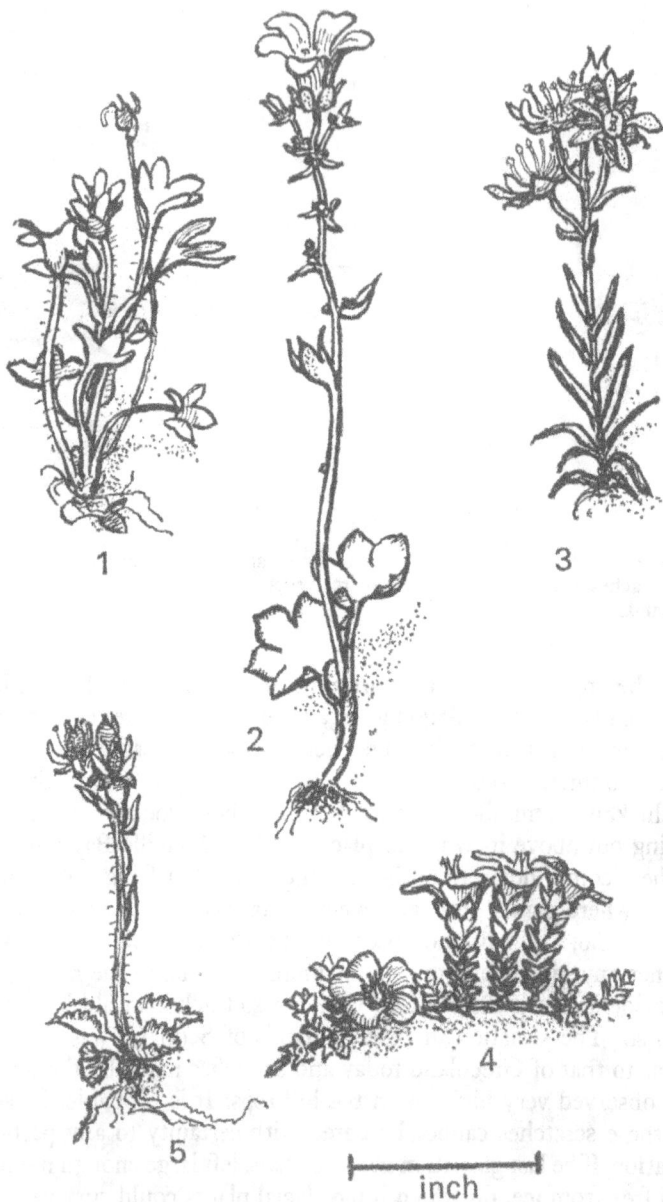

Figure 11 Saxifrages from the Alps; the Arctic and Britain, where they just survive. 1. *rivularis* (white). 2. *cernua* (white). 3. *aizoides* (yellow). 4. *oppositifolia* (rose-red). 5. *nivalis* (white). All from Greenland specimens.

them until you had climbed up to that height. But certain others, equally arctic and alpine in character, are found in other mountains right down into England and Wales (fig. 11.3, 4). Not long ago too, in 1951, a friend of mine, C. F. Tebbutt, walking on a hill near Loch Shiel at a height of only about 2,500 ft came upon a large patch of a plant, *Diapensia lapponica*, which is arctic in character and had never been found in this country before. There are also complete gaps in the Alp–Scottish mountains–Arctic distribution map.

However, as I have already suggested, the land available during an Ice Age for plants to grow on does not only include the high tops; it also includes a coastal strip, which would undoubtedly be more important for plant survival than the hills inside the ice sheet. There is another point too. Many alpine plants and arctic plants also grow perfectly well as rock plants in innumerable gardens. It does not seem as if the factor of cold, by itself, has any say in the matter, except in so far as it may discourage the growth of other plants, in particular, grasses, which might smother our alpines, nor does the factor of altitude. The preference for a particular soil is evidently as important as either. Take, for instance, *Dryas octopetala* (fig. 12.1). This is common in the Alps at 4–7,000 ft. It is known in the Snowdon range, northwards in the hills, is quite plentiful just above the shore at Keoldale near Cape Wrath in Sutherland, and widespread in Greenland. In the Alps it is particularly common on limestone. Keoldale is limestone and so also is the old glacial coastal belt. The limestone here seems to be the key factor in its survival in Britain. When we find a plant like *Dryas* surviving both on the hill-tops and on the coast, while it does not occur in between these zones, it is surely evidence that something has killed it off in between. In Greenland it is plentiful because of the lack of competition. *Ranunculus glacialis* (fig. 12.2) however, though common in the Alps and in Jan Mayen, is not found in Britain. I did not find it in Greenland. This is an attractive purplish-red flower, which I believe has not been grown in nurseries. In Jan Mayen it grows low down on volcanic soil. In the Alps it grows at an altitude of 7–12,000 ft, preferring volcanic soil also. What happened in between Switzerland and Jan Mayen? The white alpine butterwort (fig. 8.1) is now so rare in Scotland that no one knows whether it still exists.

There is the tiny, mountain azalea Loiseleuria, or *Azalea procumbens* (fig. 12.4), which is found high in the Alps, on high bare Scottish mountain tops and low down in West Greenland, or the better-known, though hardly so minute and graceful, moss campion, *Silene acaulis* (fig. 12.3). This, like *Dryas*, is found both in the Alps and the Arctic, but in Britain not only on mountain tops from Snowdon northwards

Figure 12 Plants which have survived an Ice Age? 1. *Dryas*. 2. *Ranunculus glacialis*. 3. *Silene acaulis*. 4. *Loiseleuria procumbens*. 5. *Lithospermum purpureo-caeruleum*. 1, 3 and 4 from Greenland. 2 from Jan Mayen. 5 from Devon.

but also on the Scottish coastal fringe. We have seen it growing in crannies of the basalt lava flows on the island of Canna, where the sea is so warm that rock-pools are full of pink corals.

However not all these arctic-alpine survivors are found on mountains, or on the coastal strip. There is a delightful white, honey-scented member of the azalea family, known in English as Labrador tea (fig. 9.4), surviving in very small numbers on bogs in the north of England and in Scotland. This seems to be a similar case to that of the small Greenland rhododendron (fig. 9.3), *R. lapponicum*, of which I found a single example apparently being crowded out by a large heath, *Phillodoce caerulea* (fig. 9.2), which is itself an almost vanished rarity in Scotland, though common in Norway and the Alps.

The last example which I shall mention in a list which could be greatly extended is the oyster plant, *Mertensia maritima* (fig. 9.5). This is not an alpine, for it grows on shingle just above the tide mark. If it is a survivor from before the Ice Age, then it belongs to the coastal strip only; and it appears to be dying out. It can be seen here and there in the west, and in the Scottish islands, and also in the Arctic from Jan Mayen to West Greenland. Since little else but scurvy grass grows on spray-drenched shingle, no overcrowding factor can account for its gradual disappearance. But there does seem to be less of it than there used to be. It is attractive with lovely, pale blue flowers, and is a comparatively close relation to Heavenly Blue, *Lithospermum purpureo-caeruleum* (fig. 12.5), which is also a rarity in southern Britain. I have only seen it on the edge of the cliff at Weston in East Devon.

It is interesting to discover that quite a number of beetles are also comparatively closely confined, both to hill-tops and the coastal fringe. I believe the same is true of spiders. Of course beetles can move about with ease and if they have survived the Ice Age, as seems probable, on the summits and in the islands, it is not surprising to find them too at lower levels today. Few of them are attractive to look at, although a predator named *Carabus arvensis* (fig. 4.2) is of fair size and the colour of burnished copper. But there is one beautiful species, oval and striped lengthwise in shining rainbow colours, *Chrysomela cerealis*, which in Britain is scarcely found except on some of the peaks of the Snowdon range. I have never been on Snowdon at the right time to find *Chrysomela cerealis*, but *Chrysomela fastuosa* (fig. 4.6) seems to be more common on the coastal fringe than elsewhere and will do as an illustration for the rarer species. Now if you find a specimen of a very rare beetle in the south of England it may, like a butterfly, have been blown over from the Continent. But if you find a breeding community only on the summits of a few mountains this can hardly be the case.

49

Figure 13 The coastal strip during an Ice Age. Turnstone beach, Ellesmere Island. This is the only patch of grass for many miles and is only there because the Eskimos for many centuries scattered rubbish from their winter houses, seen in the foreground. Ice still fast to the shore. Pack-ice outside.

It must be a little pocket of survivors from something. In this case *Chrysomela cerealis* seems to have persisted since the last inter-glacial period and been cut off from its Continental brothers by the ice sheet.

If we suppose that these plants I have mentioned are survivors from the Ice Age, then we can surely assume that they were very widespread and hardy plants in the last inter-glacial period. They withstood a terrible shock. I have seen the Arctic coastal strip far up beyond Smith's Sound between Greenland and the Canadian islands. On the shore of Ellesmere Island (fig. 13) nothing grew at all for miles at a time except a single species of campion, *Melandrium apetalum* (fig. 9.1). However, at a place which we named Turnstone Beach there were the remains of an old Eskimo settlement which had been occupied on and off for perhaps a thousand years. The ground beneath the grass was deeply frozen, but when it thawed a little in the summer the grass could germinate and send its roots into the rich mixture of soot and animal oil which the Eskimos had left behind. Presumably just as many grass seeds were blown on either side of the Eskimo village, but they never germinated because the soil was too poor.

Here we have two plants, a campion and a grass. One, by the accidental agency of man, grows luxuriantly in part of one small bay. The other, with no help from man, grows sporadically in all the neighbouring bays. Nowhere on the opposite coast of Greenland was it numerous. On the other hand, many miles further south on the Canadian side, on the shores of North Devon Island, there are grass-covered plains on which we watched musk oxen feeding. Either the campion or the grass must be the fitter to survive in the struggle for existence if Darwin was right. But which is the fitter? The answer surely must be, as in the Bible story of the woman who went to heaven to face the choice of several husbands, neither. There is no absolute fitness about it. It is simply a question of which suits a given set of circumstances.

However, here we have a definite piece of evidence. Nothing except *Melandrium*, itself probably a Canadian immigrant, appears to have grown on any of these beaches until Eskimos came and enriched the soil of one of them. Then the grass seeds colonized it. One would say from this that if a land is completely in the grip of an Ice Age, nothing will probably survive. When the ice goes, the whole land has to be completely recolonized. This was probably the case in Britain during the fiercest glacial period, but it was not so during the last. Many plants and animals probably survived it, and these, survivors from the preceding inter-glacial period, are the ones which we find here and there on the high hills and coastal fringe today. They are slowly being overwhelmed in most places by the immigrant waves from unglaciated areas. Both our original propositions are true, although there are probably numerous surviving species, both animal and vegetable, which have recolonized our own plains and valleys and are not now recognizable as such. The theory of the survival of the fittest has nothing to say when the cold becomes too intense for anything to live.

Five

It is a great pity that the geological record can never be more than a shot-torn fragment and that the great holes in it have to be filled in by informed guesswork. It is the same of course with other subjects, such as history, anthropology and archaeology. Too many facts are lost for any of these subjects to be more than a précis based on inherent probability. Nothing can make any of them into exact sciences and the more they ape these the less convincing they become. Theology and philosophy have caught the disease with lamentable results. The reason I write this is because there is no geological evidence to show how mammals came from reptiles, if indeed they did, nor how birds turned their scales into feathers. There were real flying reptiles, but there is nothing to show that they were closely related to early forms of bird. As with the origin of all the great orders there is a complete blank in the record and each one appears to have sprung into being with no long evolution behind it. We cannot see a blennoid fish becoming an ancestral newt. We cannot see a winged lizard becoming a feathered bird with an entirely different wing structure and we cannot see a cold-blooded scaly lizard turning into a hairy mammal in however long period we give to the processes. Thousands and thousands of little mutations, we are told, did it slowly over a period of hundreds of millions of years. Yet the fossils say nothing of this hypothesis.

Of course Darwinian evolutionists would say that the skeletons of birds and mammals are unlikely to be preserved in rocks as fossils. But there is an easy answer to that. I guarantee you would find far more skeletons of mice and blackbirds in the mud at the bottom of a pool in the garden than those of newts and frogs. As for lizards, you would never find one at all. Mice and other mammals are by far the most frequent victims in ponds. They are for ever falling into water and getting drowned; and the same is true of slow-running rivers. The dredgings from a river like the Cam are full of animal bones. I have seen the skeletons of two drowned humans found in one year in two different old fenland streams. One was of the earliest Bronze Age and the other perhaps earlier than Neolithic times. The first was in the peat and the other beneath it. Such discoveries are quite common in the Fens. No! If there had been a long succession of reptiles changing into mammals, it would have been found years ago. Birds might be rarer, for they are so light and float so long that the skeletons and bones are likely to drop to pieces and become widely scattered. But skeletons of mammals are as likely or more likely to be found than those of reptiles.

The earliest known mammals are found as fossils contemporary with the last phases of the great lizards. They are described as small and undifferentiated. This apparently means that no one knows what kind of animals they really were. However, they are assumed to be the ancestors of all mammals and so of man himself. This seems to be as wide an assumption as to say that the earliest known fossil plants, the giant club-mosses of the coal measures, are the ancestors of all the plants we know today. It is an assumption based on the Darwinian theory that every living thing evolved from an earlier type by trial and error. If this theory is wrong then there is no reason to believe that these first mammals are anything more than the first known experiments by some mind to produce warm-blooded creatures. They need not have been ancestral at all and when one sees the extraordinary developments in mammalian types in the succeeding geological ages it seems most improbable that the mutation idea is correct. It is hard to believe that a whale, a bat, an elephant and a gorilla are all derived from one parent stock. But it is perfectly easy to see that they could have been evolved by planning from one original idea of mammalness. Deliberate experimenting by some external mind, who pushed the chromosomes about in the cells of embryos to fit plans already thought out, would explain everything.

The classic example, which convinces many people of the truth of evolution, is the preserved record of ancient horses. It can be shown by fossils that there was a small five-toed beast. This was succeeded by a larger four-toed one, and then one with three toes. Lastly the single-toed horse, as we know it, came into being. But take a horse and ride it too hard on a road and the two rudimentary toes try to grow again and the animal is lamed by what is known as 'splint'. The toes have been lost by devolution and not evolution. They became unnecessary on the grassy plains, which were the homes of the early true horses. The story is told that when the Eskimo women spent the winter in huts warmed by a blubber lamp they always sat on the sleeping platform with the same side towards the heat. When they fed their babies, they used the breast which was warm and the other was neglected. In time the neglected breast tended to dry up and atrophy. The observation is probably correct and, if there were any truth in the theory of natural selection, ought in time to have produced a race of single-breasted women comparable to the one-toed horses. Fortunately Eskimo houses became somewhat modernized before this lopsided Darwinian monstrosity could become established. In point of fact the inside of an Eskimo winter house was extremely hot because the entrance passage was built with a most ingenious air-lock. This is the reason why Eskimos lived naked inside it and invited visitors to take their clothes off.

The whales and dolphins are mammals. It is very hard to see what ancestral, four-legged, hairy breed could have produced them. Not only have their hind legs vanished and their front legs turned into flippers; but they have no hair and have a great fin on their backs. There are flesh-eating whales, fish-eating dolphins, the great whalebone whales which sieve plankton and naked sea-snails through an extraordinary mesh in their throats, and the large sperm whales, the cachelots, which dive to great depths to prey on the giant squids. These giant squids themselves, although well known to sailors and frequently described, were not believed to exist by professional naturalists until portions of their tentacles were found by whalemen inside the stomachs of sperm whales. The *kraken*, as it was called in Norway, is now a commonplace.

One of the most interesting, one might almost call it romantic, stories of scientific discovery concerns the family of killer whales. The common killer whale, *Orca gladiator*, is probably the most ferocious hunting beast in the world. Its only possible rival is the sea leopard of the Antarctic. Both will try to tumble men from ice floes, or out of boats, to eat them.

One day in the last century, someone brought a fragment of bone to Sir Richard Owen, one of the most celebrated students of comparative anatomy that has ever lived. The incomplete bone is said to have only been a very few inches long and is probably still preserved somewhere. Sir Richard looked at the bone and said it had belonged to a kind of whale which was not known to science. The whale was like a killer whale and he would call it *Pseudorca*, which may be translated as 'false killer whale'. Some time later a skull was found in Lincolnshire, which confirmed him in his diagnosis. There the matter rested until this century when live *Pseudorca* were seen in the Baltic. Later still two complete skeletons of *Pseudorca* were found in the Fens. Their discoverer, Dr J. O. Garrood, a friend of mine, told me that they had evidently swum up the river from the sea until they became stuck in the mud where they died and were covered up with silt and so preserved.

A number of years after this, a large school of live 'false killers' came ashore among the northern Scottish islands. They were exactly like Owen's description. This was not the end. A couple of years later a second school of these whales was stranded in Walvis Bay, South Africa, showing how comparatively sketchy is the naturalist's knowledge of what is in the sea today. Giant squid, 'false killer' and coelacanth have all appeared alive in defiance of professional belief, and we may expect with some confidence that such things as the monsters of Scotland and Ireland will follow them in due time.

However, the point is this. The members of the whale family frequently run ashore and die there. When they do so on a muddy beach, they stand a good chance of being preserved as fossils. Why therefore is there no long geological story of their evolutionary history? What is known of the evolutionary story is really one of devolution. No existing whales have teeth divided into groups like those of other mammals. Their teeth are all alike. However there are some fossil whales of America, known as archaeoceti (ancient whales), which have their teeth divided into incisors, canines and molars. The rudiments of their hind limbs remain in their bodies, but give the appearance of having atrophied and dropped off. The most that remains is a short stump of thigh bone attached to the pelvic girdle.

Whales have remarkably solid ear bones to withstand the pressure of the water when diving deep. They are shaped much like cowrie shells. Such bones are found as fossils in this country and contemporary with extinct fossil elephants known as Mastodon. One wonders, if Darwinian evolution is true, how many whales burst their ears before this form of protection was evolved! But whales are a very poor advertisement for the theory.

The later story of whales seems to be chiefly one of devolution. The seal family appears to be at the beginning of such a story. They still have four limbs, and finger nails still remain on their digits. They still have fur and a completely recognizable set of carnivorous teeth, incisors, canines, pre-molars and molars. Zoologists set a great store by the teeth of mammals and, in fact, distinguish man from the apes by them. Some of the seals' molar teeth seem to be devolving into pegs.

If it were not for the teeth, seals would seem to be not very different from polar bears, or other beasts which are more or less amphibian. Seals, unlike whales, have to come ashore to breed. There seems to be no recent evolution at all in the seal family. They are devolving from land animals.

It is not necessary to try to study the evolution of numerous mammals. However it is interesting to see what say man has had in all this, with his experiments in breeding domestic animals and study of genetics. I think the most remarkable is the case of the domestic dog. We must remember that according to definition a species cannot produce a fertile offspring when crossed with another. It may produce mules. This has been done with such things as lions crossed with tigers and so on. But these mules cannot reproduce. Man has produced an amazing range of dog breeds, from salukis to dachshunds and bull-dogs to pekinese, but they can all breed together and produce fertile offspring. Five thousand years ago there were already many differenti-ated breeds, and beasts like whippets and terriers were kept in Britain.

Students of the dog have suggested that it came from at least two ancestral types, the wolf and an asiatic wild dog. It is known that the husky breed originated in cross-breeding with captive wolf cubs. It is most difficult to distinguish the skeleton of a large dog from that of a wolf.

When I first took up archaeology, there used to be a skull promi-nently displayed on one of the museum shelves and a barbed and tanged Bronze Age flint arrow-head sticking in the brain case. This was regarded as a classic example of the dangers confronting early man. He had evidently shot a wild wolf. One day I took the skull out and examined it. Now it is not difficult to tell the difference made on bone by a flint object and a metal one. The cut made by flint shows striations on the bone, and the metal cut is smooth. The arrow-head fitted loosely in the skull and the cut was considerably longer than the greatest breadth of the flint. Also the cut was quite smooth; it had been made by metal. I took it to our curator, Louis Clarke, and said, 'I'm sorry, Louis, but this is a fake. Disregarding the kind of cut, the arrow-head is much too small for the wound.' Louis was not pleased and in fact refused to remove the skull from the show-case. Some years later we had a visit from that celebrated Dutch professor, Van Giffen. Amongst other things he asked to look at the skull. He handled it for a moment and then said 'This is not a wolf, it is a dog. I have examined very many wolf skulls.' That ended that.

However, the point is this. Man through the ages, for eight thousand years perhaps, has been changing the bodily shapes of dogs out of all recognition, but he has not produced separate species. A wolf could still get fertile offspring from a dachshund. Just as the shapes of domestic dogs have been changed greatly through selective breeding, so big alterations have taken place with sheep. I have taken an interest in this for many years, collecting suitable bones from excavations. There were three breeds of sheep brought into Britain by the early settlers. All had remarkably thin leg and foot bones. These features remained permanently all through Bronze Age, Iron Age, Saxon, Viking and Early Mediaeval times; but a change took place apparently in the later Middle Ages, possibly due to the influence of the Crusades. Now all sheep have foot bones almost twice as wide as those of the earlier breeds, with the sole exception of the sheep from St Kilda, the Soay sheep, which look like a completely different species both in build and colour. How then are we to suppose that small mutations produced separate species? Surely the fertility business is outside the range of small mutations? A species is fixed by somebody who plans that species, however much man may alter its shape. Man may breed a useful cross between a horse and a donkey, but it will not reproduce itself as a permanent species. This is something which had to be done outside this three-dimensional world. A breed of dogs can be bred true for many generations. But introduce another breed and at once you spoil the sequence. I have no doubt that in a few generations you could reverse the process and breed back to the original wolves, as has been done with horses and cows in Germany.

The same story is to be found in the botanical world. For many thousands of years man has been cultivating food plants. But however much he can improve on a grain, or a vegetable, he cannot cross them so as to produce a new species. A grapefruit is not a new species, but a mule.

Of course this is of great importance to man if he is worried about his ancestry. Darwin definitely stated that he was descended from an ancestral monkey, an early form of gibbon, tail and all. As time went on it was seen that Darwin's idea could not have worked and man's ancestor has now been put back to some primitive kind of lemur.

A vast amount of work has gone into this study. Men have gone all over the world searching for what was once known as the 'missing link'. Quite a large number of different kinds of fossil man have been found causing controversy to rage and hoaxes to be perpetrated. But, in spite of all this effort, fossil men are still men, monkeys are still monkeys and lemurs still lemurs. The more prolonged the study is, the less likely it becomes that any missing links will ever be found. Man appeared on earth as man, with his toes as they are today and not with his big toe on the opposite side of his foot. He always walked upright in spite of the former belief that Neanderthal man crept about in a hunched position. This idea has now gone into the limbo with many others. In fact it seems probable now that Neanderthal man could produce fertile offspring with the so-called Homo sapiens, which is us. Bit by bit the Darwinian idea of the origin of man is being shown to have been impossible. Yet the idea at the back of it all still remains unquestioned, because the thought of questioning it is never put into the heads of young people. They grow up to look on it as a proved article of faith.

Before we leave this part of the book, we will take a very brief look at another great natural order, the birds. As I said before, birds are so light that it is not easy for them to be preserved as complete, or even partially complete, fossils. But one really early bird has been found with most of its feathers still showing plainly in the rock. This bird is called the archaeopteryx. Most of it was like a modern bird, although it lived in a world of monstrous dinosaurs and of flying lizards with wings in some cases 18 ft in span. Despite the fact that evolutionists would like to derive birds from lizards, it is very clear that the wings of the first known birds were quite different from those of the ptero-dactyls, the name by which the flying lizards as a family are known. Their wings were membranes spread between fingers and more like those of the bats. The skeletons of the early birds, however, were more or less on the same general plan as lizards as a whole. But they were covered with feathers and had feathers spaced laterally all down a long tail. There is not the slightest hint anywhere of a missing link between lizards and birds, although one would have expected very many early mutations between the two orders to have crashed into water and have been preserved as fossils. The first to be found is a bird pure and simple. How feathers can have been formed by mutation just isn't known. It seems most improbable that it could have happened like that. It is easier to imagine that both hair and feathers were completely new ideas added to a generalized lizard body. It was Thomas Huxley, Darwin's protagonist, who postulated that birds came from lizards. But it was Sir Richard Owen in 1862, five years earlier, who had demonstrated that the archaeopteryx was not, as had formerly been supposed, a feathered flying reptile, but a genuine bird. It now forms the first family in the class of *Aves*, the birds.

All modern birds differ from the archaeopteryx in several ways, but the most obvious is that the tail bones have almost vanished. This is not evolution but devolution. Although birds may have very long tails today, this is not due to a jointed bony structure; it is simply due to the relative length of the feathers. These are little related to a rudimentary tail, but grow from a muscular pad, known to the vulgar as 'the parson's nose'. Although a magpie today looks, when flying away from us, much like an animated windmill, the archaeopteryx can hardly have flown like a bird at all. Its steering must have been very inefficient when compared with the brilliant flight evolutions of modern birds and it obviously could not stop with the beautiful exactitude of a seagull landing on the truck of a mast. Modern birds have a mastery of the air quite beyond that of their supposed earliest ancestor. If you have heard a pigeon crashing through the trees, it is absolutely nothing compared with what must have happened when an archaeopteryx came in to land. So the long bony tail had to go; but who told the genes, which had built the tail, that they were no longer required? This is the crux of the whole matter. Even if a series of small accidental changes could make an organism develop in a particular manner; could they then, when a certain point is reached, order that organism to get rid of some of the organs which had been gradually built up? Surely we are assuming an advanced mentality for the genes, which nobody has any reason to expect. Little notice appears to have been taken of the devolutionary side of the story; but to produce an efficient animal you have to postulate both evolution and devolution, not once, but many times.

I will not deal with bird migration here, but one other point should be made. Our cuckoo, but not all cuckoos, deposits its eggs in the nests of smaller birds, one at a time. When an egg hatches, the other eggs, or young birds in the nest, cause intensive irritation to a spot on the young cuckoo's back between the growing wings. The young bird struggles to rid itself of this irritation and manages to heave up each egg or bird between its shoulders until it has pushed them out of the nest and has it all to itself. All young birds fidget in their nests of course, but what chance series of mutations produced this spot on the young cuckoo's back, so that it would be forced to turn the other little birds out and ensure a big enough food supply for itself alone? The foster parents could never have managed to feed the whole brood. A young cuckoo takes all the time they have to give. I have watched the development of a cuckoo in a sedge warbler's nest beside the Loddon as a boy and been disgusted at its greed. It ended up many sizes larger than its elegant and beautiful foster parents.

Part Two

Six

There is little sense in trying to refute a theory unless you have some idea to put in its place. The object of all research is to try to add to human knowledge, and it is the duty of everyone who does such research to make his results known. For several years now my wife and I have been working on an unorthodox subject and I have published the results in a series of popular books: *Ghost and Ghoul, Ghost and Divining Rod, E.S.P.* and *A Step in the Dark.* Now I am going to summarize some of the results we obtained, with the addition of some discoveries we have made since these reports were written, and to see whether they throw some light on the subject of evolution. They may not throw a great deal of light; but I think they do provide a basis from which a great deal more might be found out, and amply justify my preceding assault on a widely-held, and I think highly dangerous, dogma. But readers must not assume that I have said here all that is to be learnt in the other four books: and these in themselves do no more than scratch at the surface of a vast subject.

There is no doubt that belief in extra-sensory perception is becoming wider every year and that more is written about it and more understood than ever before. Some forms of it, such as hypnosis and telepathy, are now orthodox subjects; although it is not known how they work. Water divining, and even divining for oil and metals, is now widely employed. But other branches, such as psychometry, are still looked on with doubt and suspicion by most scientists and indeed by that section of humanity which considers itself educated and intellectual. As for ghosts and apparitions, half the world denies, often furiously, that they could exist, although they see them every day on their television screens.

Now, we began our studies on these subjects with a completely open mind. If anything it was inclined towards disbelief. As we progressed we felt doubts at every step and frequently returned to the beginning again to see whether we could see flaws in our observation or our reasoning. After years of work we still handle any information which we have not obtained ourselves with the care with which I was taught to touch a stick of gelignite. We know we are dealing with as tenuous and difficult a subject as any that exists and are never carried away with enthusiasm.

To begin with it seemed probable that we were dealing with what should have been a branch of psychology; but there was obviously more to it than that, for we discovered that we could find objects buried underground which were, in the nature of themselves, concrete. Buried pins, spoons, buttons, beads, nails and potsherds are tangible evidence. But there was also the discovery of a mass of subjective material which could not be obtained by any known means and yet could be shown to be correct. I think perhaps that we might say that we are dealing with a psychological study, but that it is one which professional psychologists have not tackled in a scientific manner. It goes, in fact, far beyond anything they have yet touched.

Now, there is no space in this book to go over in any detail the work which has been published in those which preceded it. To a large extent therefore I shall be compelled to make statements without the evidence on which they are based. However I am most anxious that nobody should accept them without making their own tests. Most people can do this if it is only by using a cotton-reel on a length of cotton. It can be shown that those who cannot do this usually give an unsatisfactory reaction for their nervous system. E.s.p. is a faculty all should possess and most, if not all, animals do use it.

The investigation was set in train here by the appearance of a ghost near a house at the bottom of the hill below us. Seeking for an explanation of why an apparently normal human figure should be seen in broad daylight when it could be shown that there was no such figure there, I began with the idea that it might be in the nature of a television picture held in some static electro-magnetic field. Since I had known for many years that I could use a divining rod, and suspecting that this was operated by coming in contact with such fields, I thought this might be a simple way of investigating them. It did not take long to find out that the divining rod reacted to fields around trees, about running water, sheets of roofing iron and even around human beings themselves. The original object of the investigation became quickly lost in the general interest of the subject. What were these fields and why should one be able to detect their presence with a bit of twig?

Now a divining rod is hardly an instrument of precision. Although it would demonstrate and give a rough idea of the shape of a field around an object, it is impossible to tell within inches where the point of the fork is when it begins to rotate. I therefore exchanged the rod for that other stand-by of the diviner, the pendulum. Divining is now widely known as dowsing, although this is not a very attractive term. The subject as a whole has been christened 'radiaesthesia', in itself a somewhat confusing term. The old name of divination is as good as any. It is, of course, a kind of magic.

When I decided to practise divination, I simply cut a 1 inch sphere off the top of an old walking stick; pegged two yards of thread into it with a match and fastened the other end to a short cylindrical rod, which could be rolled around between one's finger and thumb and so raise or lower the ball on the thread. This was the pendulum which I have used ever since.

Many dowsers use a pendulum for various purposes, but few do so in the same manner as we do. I got the idea many years ago from a pamphlet by some French brigadier whose name I have forgotten. He claimed to have been able to find enemy mines in the sea by swinging a pendulum with the correct length of thread on it, and pointing with his other index finger. He obtained the correct length of thread by tuning in over a sample object on the floor and lengthening the pendulum cord until it gyrated. Presumably he found the mines by tuning in over a piece of iron to obtain what is known as the 'rate' for iron. I shall use the term 'rate' a great deal and it is as well to be sure what this means. A pendulum rate is the length of cord between the top of the 'bob', the ball, and the bottom of the rod used as a windlass. In practice it can be shown that everything, whether concrete, or abstract, has one or more rates. Colours, metals, trees, insects, points of the compass, life, light and so on have their rates. It is no more difficult to find the rate of, shall we say, anger, than it is to find that of copper. You simply have to think of something which makes you feel angry, swing the pendulum back and forth, and lower the ball down until it gyrates. When it does, you have the rate for anger. It will always be the same.

There has been a house on this site at Hole for at least seven hundred years. Judging by the occasional scraps of Roman pottery which I dig up around it, there has been occupation here, although it may have been interrupted, for nearly double that time. Therefore it is not surprising that the soil around the house is full of trivial objects of antiquity. The soil is mostly covered by small lawns. When therefore I decided to research with the pendulum and found that I could obtain the rates of various objects, I chose to follow the old French brigadier's example by looking for hidden objects beneath the turf near the house.

The method is perfectly easy. You find the rate for a given substance in the way I have described. Then you measure off that rate on the pendulum cord. You go to the area to be searched and start the pendulum swinging gently back and forth. While it is swinging you extend your other arm with the forefinger pointing and move it slowly horizontally like a radar scanner. The movement must be slow and you must watch the pendulum. If your moving finger passes over a spot where an object of the required type lies hidden underground, you will notice a hesitation in the swing of the pendulum. At this point, stop moving the finger. The pendulum will now go into a circular swing and looking along the pointing finger you have a line of bearing on the hidden object, which you can mark out with small sticks, or anything convenient. Now move away to some distance, a few yards will do if you are in a confined space, and repeat the process till you get a second gyration on the pendulum. You now have a second line of bearing on the object and where the two lines intersect that object lies hidden in the ground. In practice your bearing will not be very exact, but the position can be then found within an inch or two. You no longer point, but approach the crossing point with the pendulum swinging. Close to the point it will go into a circular swing. Mark it on the ground and repeat the process half a dozen times or more. You will find a circle marked out on the ground. Directly beneath the central point is the object. When done with care, this evolution is astonishingly exact. As with anything else the operator improves greatly with practice, and gets to know the feel of the pendulum and the speed at which to move his finger; but in the very first afternoon I found several objects beneath the lawn.

After some weeks of work, it became apparent that we had already found one axiom: the radius of the circle around a given small object will always be equal to the pendulum rate for that object. It is convenient to call whatever surrounds the object its 'field'; but it is by no means certain that it is a field. However we will leave that problem for a moment.

It also became clear that, unlike what is found in chemistry, a compound of several elements did not have a rate of its own, but a rate for each element of which it was composed. Even the rates of trace elements were easily detected with the pendulum. This might have been expected to offer a quick method of discovering the chemical composition of a compound. But it is not so easy. Not only do several elements have the same rate. For instance lead, silver, calcium and sodium all react to the rate of 22 inches. But chalk, calcium carbonate, besides giving its own rates for calcium, carbon and oxygen, also appears to take up those of any metals with which it has been in contact. This can be extremely tiresome. There is a type of coarse pottery found round here and probably of Late Saxon, or Early

Norman date. The clay from which it was baked had been mixed with small pieces of chalk, as is frequently found with such coarse pottery, sand, bits of shell and even grass being used sometimes. When testing a known buried rubbish heap with the pendulum, I had a fix at one spot for what appeared to be a gold and copper object. I expected to find a Norman piece of gilded copper. Instead, when at last the thing was found, it proved to be a fragment of this coarse pottery only about an inch long. I find that a small chalk pit on top of the hill gives both these reactions. The induction of external rates on a substance is going to be of great importance later on in the story, but at this stage of the investigation it was a nuisance. Except in very obvious cases I do not think that the pendulum can be used as an alternative method of chemical analysis, nor yet as a cure-all for careless archaeological excavation. It certainly could and should be used to check what unobservant diggers have left behind on their rubbish heaps. No enthusiastic boy could have come behind the excavators of the Temple of Mithras and found a whole museum case full of interesting objects had a pendulum been used before the work was declared finished. I am perfectly certain that I have left many things behind in past excavations, which could have been found had I known how to use a pendulum. There is no excuse now. If someone comes after an excavation and picks up a brooch which might have dated the whole thing, only the excavator is to blame. In many parts of the country even flint implements can be found in this way, though it is not worth trying where there is flint in the soil.

This first excursion into divination opened a field full of surprises. First it showed that measurement could be applied to magic and then that magic could reveal concrete objects, which owing to the nature of their position, were completely concealed from the operation of the five human senses, sight, hearing, taste, smell and touch. These objects could be and often were so small, minute pins, glass beads or lace tags, that clearly the performance was most sensitive. It was also, when properly conducted, very exact. As I said before, everybody ought to be able to do this and most people can; but some have too little power, current, vital force, or whatever it is and this can be shown, when we get further with the story, to be due, in part at any rate, to some inadequacy in the nervous system.

Having demonstrated to our own and many other people's satisfaction that much could be revealed by divination, it then became necessary to see what form the supposed fields around objects took. It was expected that the fields would be spherical, but it was soon found that they extended upwards far above each object. By placing an object on the floor at ground level, plotting the circle around it with markers and repeating the process on the floor above, it was shown that the ascending field was a long and narrow cone. By placing the object upstairs and doing it all over again we could see that a similar cone proceeded downwards also. The complete field was a pair of cones joined together at a base in the horizontal plane about the object. It was also demonstrated that these cones were not rigid and that their apices, at any rate, moved around in a small ellipse according to the time of day. This has not been sufficiently studied, but the movement does not appear to be due to the rotation of the earth in relation to the sun. It may be due to the moon.

Here it is necessary to put in a few remarks which are not observed fact, but theory. What makes the pendulum gyrate? I think it is evident that when you swing it you yourself send out some ray or beam by means of its vibration. This vibration is regulated by the length of the cord. But, as I hope to show later, the vibration is higher than anything known to three-dimensional science. The ray can be directed by the pointer, in this case an index finger, although a light stick is more effective at a distance. The ray sweeps round like a radar scanner. At a given point it meets the narrow vertical field, which in itself may be a ray, from an object which has the rate which, by testing over a specimen, can be shown to repel it. The back and forth movement changes into a circular swing because the ray from the object will not let it pass and turns it back on itself. You are still sending out your ray, so, on meeting the obstruction, all that the swinging pendulum can do is to turn back on itself. Since it is held at the point of suspension, it must go round and round again. There is nothing strange about this and it could be demonstrated mechanically. Even a bullet ricochets from a steel plate.

What, then, is the process at the receiving end of the bullet? The steel plate, on being struck, vibrates and (amongst other things) sends out a cone of sound waves. There are other waves, of course, too, heat for instance. Now we have only assumed that we were investigating fields of force, biconical fields of great height and little breadth based on the object examined. But suppose that instead of a field of force around it you are really dealing with a bundle of vertical rays emanating from that object. When you hit the object with your ray the object will vibrate backwards and forwards and draw a very acute double triangle with each apex on the vertical bundle of rays. From whatever side you approach the object with the pendulum you will get the same effect. If two people do this at almost the same time they will get two sets of double triangles and so on. There may well be no biconical field of force at all, but only vertical rays. I think that this is the correct answer—but I may well be wrong. I have no training in this kind of reasoning. What is needed here is a competent and imaginative student of harmonics. Whether I am wrong or right, however, one further point is clear. The point where the two rays meet must be at the object itself, for only in the horizontal plane around the object is the circle at its greatest diameter and the radius of that circle is always of equal length to the rate of the pendulum itself. For this reason if the object is deep underground you can calculate how far this is by measuring the radius of the circle formed on the surface of the ground, and relating this to the shape of the cone. From an archaeological point of view this information is not of great value unless the object is several feet underground. But in estimating the depth of minerals it could be of some importance. Tables could easily be worked out to give precise figures.

So far we appear to have shown beyond any doubt that we possess a faculty outside those officially ascribed to humanity and that this faculty comes within reach of scientific study. Magic it may be, but in this case magic ceases to be superstitious nonsense and becomes a practical subject. Have we any idea of the type of ray which is sent out? For not only do we send a ray out ourselves, but every object appears to be emitting one all the time.

I gave what I think must be the answer to this question in my last book, *A Step in the Dark*. In this I described how, when the B.B.C. sent down a unit here in August 1966 to make a film about our experiments, I was wired for sound and connected with a tape-recorder in another room. On being asked to pick up and hold a divining rod, the needle on the dial of the sound-recorder at once jumped up far above the range of human hearing and stuck there. It was clear that the divining rod through my agency was sending out a very high sound vibration. It is, in fact, a kind of tuning-fork. It is only an assumption that the pendulum when oscillating—that is, swinging backwards and forwards—does the same. But it is a reasonable assumption because it functions in a similar way to the divining rod.

Of course if we are dealing with what is sometimes and incorrectly known as ultra-sonic sound (you cannot of course have sound beyond sound) then many natural phenomena are explained. The reason for the elaborate ears of bats must be in order that they can hear ultra-sonic rays inaudible to ordinary ears. But presumably the whiskers of animals and the antennae of insects are divining rods or radar scanners for the same purpose.

Further examination of what we had been calling 'fields' led to a somewhat clearer idea of their character. It could be demonstrated that a larger object of irregular shape did not have a neat circle round it on the perimeter of which the pendulum reacted. The shape of the outline was itself irregular conforming to that of the object inside it. This suggests that large numbers of vertical rays proceeded upwards and down from every part of the substance. Since very minute objects can be detected by their rays, the inference is that a ray proceeds from every small particle of an object. Perhaps in the case of inanimate objects these would come from molecules, and in living matter from the cells. This is, of course, highly conjectural.

Now we will return again from speculation to observed fact. Experiment had shown that it was possible, and indeed easy, to locate and subsequently excavate objects lost long ago in the soil beneath a sheet of turf. However we now go a stage beyond this. Gold, of course, has a fascination of its own. Every digger hopes to find it. However in my whole archaeological life I have only four times found gold. Twice I dug up Anglo-Saxon gold pendants, once a number of tiny strips from a piece of gold brocade; and once a gold coin, an angel of Edward IV. Ancient gold objects are not common in this country and even gold coins of any antiquity are rare, although I once had the good fortune to buy in for the Cambridge Museum a gold coin of the Roman emperor Honorius, of the early fifth century, which had just been dug out of a ditch beside the road outside Huntingdon. Very few gold coins of Honorius, the last emperor of Britain, have ever been found in this country. In spite of its scarcity, the urge to attempt to find gold is considerable and I had to try the pendulum around the house. To my surprise I soon got a reaction on the 29 inch rate for gold, but on excavating the spot uncovered the larva of a beetle. I will not go into this further here, but various things suggested that I had accidentally stumbled on the rate for femininity. Numerous tests over male and female subjects showed that this idea is correct. The rate for female is 29 inches and the same as that for gold. The male rate was found later after considerable difficulty. It is 24 inches and the same as that of diamond. The rate for diamond is exactly double that of carbon of which it is composed.

The discovery that male and female had rates on the pendulum was a great surprise; although one should have remembered that pendulums have been used to sex eggs and unborn babies for a very long time indeed. It is not difficult to understand that rays proceed from concrete objects and that they can be perceived by a super-sonic ray proceeding from an investigator. But here we appear to make contact with a different kind of ray, not one proceeding from something we can touch and see, but something far less tangible. What is sex? It is certainly not tangible in the sense that a bead or a pin is tangible. Yet the pendulum told the truth about concrete objects and did so again whenever the rates for sex were tried out on living organisms. It seems that it has to be accepted that the pendulum can identify intangibles also. Intangibles must have their own particular rays.

This was soon shown experimentally. The sex rates were found to persist in the skulls of dead birds, fishes and mammals, but only in the skulls. The pelvic bones, which might have been assumed to be connected with sex, gave no reaction. It was found that sex rates persisted in certain fossil sea urchins presumed to be something like two hundred million years old; but not in most of the contemporary fossil molluscs. It seemed that the rate only persisted if it had once been enclosed in a box-like structure, in a brain case, or a sea urchin's 'test'. In the molluscs the animal lives outside its box. It would seem almost that sex urges set up vibrations which, when enclosed, persisted in what enclosed them for two hundred million years and could then be detected with a pendulum. This is a difficult mouthful to swallow.

But worse problems were to follow. Experiment showed that any dead animal, or any part of a dead animal, always responded to a rate of 40 inches. It was so constant, and missing from live animals, that it appeared that this rate could only be that of death. Twenty inches was found to be found without exception in all living animals. This rate must stand for life. But the life rate was found in all dead animals also. It did not vanish when the animal died.

Here are two pieces of information which appear to point to something completely different from anything known to science. Some sense we have seems to be able to get in touch not only with objects which are obscured from us; it can also contact vibrations whose originators have been dead two hundred million years. That is so long ago that we might just as well say that the duration of the vibrations is endless. The pendulum also appears to say that life vibrations pass beyond death. This seems quite absurd to anyone brought up to a materialistic or rationalist outlook; yet there is no difference in the manner in which the pendulum reacts to the two kinds of phenomena. If one set can be proved by the finding of solid objects whose position and even existence could not be guessed through a blanket of soil, then there is no valid reason for assuming that the other set of answers is not correct. It seems more probable that the materialistic outlook is based on inadequate knowledge of fact. Still we will leave this point for the moment and go on to see what other surprises the pendulum has in store for us. There are many.

Once it becomes clear that abstract phenomena, such as life and death, have rates, there is no limit. The rate for any thought concept can be found easily by simply thinking of it and lowering the pendulum until it gyrates. 'Anger' can be found by thinking of something which annoys you. It has a rate of 40 inches, the same as death. 'Evolution' is obtained by some method such as visualizing the supposed development of fish to amphibians. It is 36 inches. Devolution comes on the same rate as undifferentiated sex at 16 inches. This sounds most improbable and even crazy. However if the divining rod works by using ultra-sonic sound, all the pendulum is now telling us is that every major thought form has a special ultra-sonic note of its own. This is no longer absurd, but simply a piece of information we did not have before.

Of course this is taking us into that horrible world of thinking where we are told that if you see a glass of beer on a table there is not the slightest evidence that there is a glass of beer, or a table. We merely think they exist because a number of little electric circuits operate to send impressions into a computer, which is our brain, and give our mind a picture of a glass of beer. Science too tells us that the glass of beer is almost entirely empty space, a kind of series of holes joined together by very little. The beer isn't even yellow. According to the scientist it is every other colour except yellow. This in terms of the pendulum would be purple, but we have not got as far as that yet.

I do not wish to become involved in these complications. For our purpose it is every bit as sensible to say that all thought forms have an extremely high sound vibration which we can contact with a pendulum, as it is to say that when we see and drink a glass of beer it isn't there at all. To the ordinary person this is utter bunkum. We are given our senses to use and enjoy the glass of beer, whether it is really a glass of beer or not. Therefore I see, much as I doubted it at first, that you can find thoughts with a pendulum. Furthermore the pendulum appears to tell us that a thought once made continues indefinitely. The sex thoughts of Cretaceous sea urchins can still be contacted. I think this is the same as saying that thought is timeless and that experience exists independently of the person who experienced it.

Seven

I hope this chapter will not be as difficult as the last. Whatever I am writing about I try to make as simple as possible, for I know how easily I myself am bored by complicated reading. However this whole study is so hard to understand that I cannot hope to make it very easy. Fortunately there are few technical terms, for the subject is in its infancy.

Quite early in the work it became clear that there were substances which did not behave in the normal manner. I have already told how chalk was found to (shall we say) echo, the rates of minerals such as gold, copper and iron, which were not in its composition at all. But there are other minerals which seem to kill the transmission of the ray dead at its source in the pendulum. Lead and calcium do this, but silver, with the same rate of 22 inches as they have, does not.

It is easy to demonstrate this property of what I call 'interruptors'. Take a small piece of lead, not graphite from a pencil, which is often called lead; the cap off a wine bottle will do. Hold the lead in the left hand. Now tune the pendulum in to the correct rate for, say, a copper object, 30·5 inches, lying on the floor. The pendulum will then go into a circular swing. Now transfer the piece of lead from the left hand to the other which is holding the gyrating pendulum. Immediately the circular movement stops and is replaced by an oscillating, backwards and forwards, movement. If you do not pass the lead from one hand to the other, but instead drop it on the floor beside the copper object, exactly the same thing happens. The pendulum swings as if it had never been tuned in at all. Yet you can find buried lead on its 22 inch rate, although it will stop the pendulum reacting to a silver object which has the same rate. The calcium in the rubies used for their bearings prevents one from finding watches by this rate method.

The reason for this obstructing effect has not yet been found. The phenomena do not apparently show that the ray is stopped from passing out of the pendulum, for directly the piece of lead is removed the circular movement begins again. What we observe is clearly the repulsion and turning back of one ray by another which gives the pendulum its circular swing. When the lead ray is added, there is no repulsion and the two rays either pass by, or through one another. We do not know why this should happen, but it explains why the pendulum is not always successful in locating things. A piece of lead, or even a snail shell (calcium) may be enough to interrupt. No doubt there are other interruptors yet to be found. There are certainly some organic ones, and others such as graphite, which reverse some rates and give male instead of female and female for male. Again this is at present incomprehensible.

Once it is apparent that thought forms, or conceptions, have their own rates, a very wide field is ready for exploration. It is in fact limitless. All the human emotions and faculties can be rated. Colours, the points of the compass, forces like electricity and light can all be found with comparative ease. But everywhere there has to be some mental discrimination in the mind of the operator. It is his ray which is being sent out and, although he is controlling it by the length of the pendulum, there are several differing concepts on each rate. For instance gold, female, yellow and danger each have a rate of 29 inches. The operator must be clear in his mind whether he wishes to contact gold, or be warned of danger. Concentrated thought however tends to damp down and spoil the whole operation.

A large number of experiments have been conducted with organic substances and living organisms. There are rates for the different families of plants and those of animals. In practice it can be observed that the same rate is found to be common to a particular family of insects and the food on which they feed. Of course a given insect will react to a number of rates. It will react for its sex, for each chemical of which its body is composed and so on. But it has what might be called a generic rate for the whole family and this is the same as that for its food. For instance, the rate for grass is 16 inches. The families of the dung beetles, such as *Aphodius* and *Geotrupes* which we have mentioned earlier in the book, have the same 16 inch rate. There is thus a common ultra-sonic note to which they all respond. Or we can take the case of *Bolboceras*, which I described in detail in my last book, *A Step in the Dark*. This very rare beetle feeds on truffles found in beech woods. A truffle grows on the mast from beech trees. An examination with the pendulum shows that the beetle, the truffle and the beech tree all have a rate of 17 inches. Not only that, but a snail feeding under beech trees, *Cyclostoma elegans*, also has the 17 inch rate.

Now, a couple of generations ago, the celebrated French naturalist, Henri Fabre, after many years devoted to the study of insects, was convinced that these were drawn to their food and their opposite sexes

74

by some intangible ray. Realizing the large numbers which were attracted to evil-smelling foods, he deduced that unsmellable smell was the source of attraction. The pendulum appears to give us a different answer. There is indeed a ray, but this ray is common to the insect and to its particular type of food. There is good reason for supposing that it is super-sonic, ultra-sonic, or whatever name you like to give to very high vibrational sound. Just as a bat, by means of its elaborate ears, can fly swiftly in the dark, avoiding all obstructions because it hears the rays coming from them, so the insect can fly direct to its food, or to its mate. It carries a built-in radar set on its head in the shape of antennae tuned directly to its own rate and that of its food. The carrion beetles, *Necrophorus* and *Silpha*, have no difficulty in finding a dead bird, for each has the built-in rate of 8 inches. *Sinodendron* lives on rotten oak and some other trees. Both oak and *Sinodendron* have a rate of 11 inches.

This apparently ultra-sonic relationship between an animal and its food suggests a degree of planning far beyond the chance of casual mutation. The rate is exact and you can measure it. Chance and 'the survival of the fittest' cannot be measured. Whatever we may think caused the animal to have the same rate as its food; whether generations of feeding on that food may have induced that rate, or what happened, the fact remains that there is a completely accurate device in the animal to tune it in to that rate. This surely implies that, whatever caused the food to be there, some mind designed the animal to feed on it. The implication is that the animal was made in order to turn waste products of the earth back into soil on which fresh things could grow.

The rates give us another hint at careful planning when we examine those of colours. It is widely known that black and yellow together spell a warning. The rates tell us why. Black, 40 inches, is on the same rate as 'death'; yellow at 29 inches is 'danger'. A wasp the sting of which can sometimes even kill a human is boldly marked with these two colours (fig. 5.2). A hornet, a much less aggressive animal has the colours toned down to brown and orange. Carrion-feeding beetles too, *Silpha* or *Necrophorous*, are frequently either black, or black and yellow. The colour black exercises a great attraction for flies, who evidently mistake its 40 inch colour rate for the 40 inch death rate. If you walk through bracken with someone dressed in black, most of the flies at once concentrate on him. It is surprizing too how many yellow flowers are poisonous. One need only mention laburnum and buttercup; laburnum with its very dangerous black seeds wears both colours. On the other hand 'purple', with a rate of 9 inches, stands apparently for

F

'safety'. Numerous purple flowers are useful herbs, or were so when herbs were used medicinally. Thyme, sage, rosemary, mint, comfrey. lavender, to name some of them, all have mauve, or purple, flowers. Even the deadly nightshade, which as belladonna is a useful drug, has a purple flower—although its deadly berry is a shining black. This purple, of course, is not the purple of classical antiquity, which was scarlet. The violet, with its purple flowers, was one of the original producers of aspirin and gives a rate of 32 inches for health as well as 9 inches for safety. One would almost think that yellow and purple had been deliberately chosen to show the safety, or otherwise, of a given plant. The 9 inch rate for purple can be found on a plant before the flowers are out. This appears to show that the safety rate is inborn in the plant itself.

One of the few really poisonous families of fish found on our coasts, the weavers, has black and yellow spiny fins near its head. These fishes carry a nasty poison in their spines. I remember a Uist fisherman being very badly stung when he accidentally picked one out of a lobster creel. But the usual victims are children paddling on sandy beaches at low-water, for the weavers hide in the sand. I do not know how many people are stung each year; but nobody seems to worry about it. There is one other fish which is said to sting, the dusky skulpin. This is yellow with blue streaks and spots. I have only once seen one caught and do not know whether it is really dangerous. But fishermen think so and it is yellow. The skulpin was bashed against the gunwale of the boat till it fell back into the sea. I remember this well, for it was the first time I was ever sea-sick. We were rolling at anchor in a Norfolk beach-boat and catching dabs on hand lines baited with hermit crabs. I hated to see the crabs treated with such brutality and had never heard of sea-sickness. It was a horrid day and the skulpin made it worse; but it did not cure my love of the sea and boats. I was quite small at the time and had been taken fishing by some foreign baron who wanted to marry my widowed mother. No doubt I was supposed to report back on how kind he had been. If so the expedition was a failure. Anyhow, nothing came of the romance. I have digressed, and digression is thought disgraceful in a serious study. But most serious books are infernally dull; in fact they are so dull that few people bother to read them.

Well then, to be serious again. So far the pendulum seems to have suggested a most remarkable idea. This is that poisonous insects, fish and plants frequently sport the colour yellow which has, so it says, the same 29 inch rate as danger. Many also have the colour black about them, and black, 40 inches, has the rate for death. Perhaps if you examined all the known yellow and black insects and fish you would get an average which said the opposite. I don't know and certainly am not going to spend a long time trying to find out. I can only point to our British examples, I can get little confirmation of the opposite, but I can get some. I know of no purple fish. But I do know that our harmless and commonest jelly-fish, *Aurelia*, has four purple rings in its colourless body, while our most poisonous species, *Cyanaea*, is yellowish brown. Conan Doyle made *Cyanaea* into a killer, but I have never heard of anyone who actually died from its stings. However his story, *The Lion's Mane*, was a good puzzle.

I can only think of one purple insect in this country. It is a harmless and rather attractive little globular beetle known as *Chrysomela goetingensis* (fig. 4.5). It is not at all common and is said to feed on thyme.

The colouring of birds seems to be outside this picture. No one could regard a canary, goldfinch or yellow hammer as dangerous, although it is perhaps significant that most of the hawks have bright yellow legs and yellow at the base of their beaks.

Most significant of all, however, are the great hunting cats, the tigers and leopards. Here, whether striped, or spotted, the marks of danger are plain for all to see.

There are still two other things on the 29 inch rate to be considered. First there is gold, a comparatively useless, but attractive metal. I always think that gold became the symbol for money because it is the colour of ripe corn. Corn was the life of the agriculturalist. But money, we are told, is the root of all evil. Greed and crime attend the search for it. Here you have your danger. The second is female sex. Well, I have a very high opinion of femininity; still the female when she has to hunt for food for her children is undoubtedly a greater killer than her mate. She has to be. This, rather than the Japanese belief that beautiful women can change into foxes, must be the reason that female responds to the rate for danger. All that the pendulum can give to the male, 24 inches, is the rate for diamond. I took a long time to find this rate, for I quite expected it to be that of something valueless like lead. There is no colour that I can find on the male rate. In this context he is quite uninteresting. Diamond is associated with male in ancient lore and so is gold with female, but I did not know this.

Somehow man recognized that black and yellow spelt danger. Before the days of Nelson ships of war were painted in variegated colours. But Nelson, who was something of a mystic as well as a great sailor, insisted that all the ships under his command be painted black and yellow. His enemies have left on record that nothing they had ever seen was so daunting as the slow approach of the two lines of British ships at Trafalgar. After the Napoleonic wars our vessels were painted black and white, which may have looked more attractive, but was not nearly so sinister.

Red on the pendulum has the rate of 10 inches. This is also the rate for youth. White and life come together at 20 inches and green with age at 30. Black and death we already know at 40. There is great significance in this grouping as I shall try to show before long, but at the moment we are dealing with colours in particular. There are many red insects and even more red and black ones. There is no obvious significance in this. But when we come to fruits and berries the edible ones are nearly all red when ripe. Even the poisonous yew tree has a red fruit cup which children eat without harm. Red, with its association with youth, therefore seems to be a given sign that the fruit is good to eat. Other edible fruits are purple for safety. Bramble, whortleberry and wild plum are obvious examples. But I have heard that the fruit of berberis is poisonous and I would not like to try it. However the flowers of berberis are either yellow or a venomous orange, which should be a warning sign. Although the elder tree has always been thought hostile to mankind, its purple berries are edible and make flavourings and wines. The chances are that these fruits are more for the eyes of birds than for humanity and that their digestions are less tender than ours.

It is noticeable how many carnivorous hunting-insects wear the black livery of death. But it is not so easy to see why so many birds and insects should be so very brightly coloured. Brilliant metallic green is a favourite colour for insects and so is a combination of green with burnished copper. Almost all colours are found in varying combinations on butterflies. These colours are obviously no assistance in the struggle for existence and might be regarded as a definite hindrance. It is also difficult to see what chance mutations produced the brilliant red, black and white pattern on the red admiral and retained it through the ages. It seems more probable that these beauties were deliberately designed by some mind for its own enjoyment and for the pleasure of others. The same seems to apply to many birds and even fishes. Many moths, however, which rest through the day, are carefully coloured to harmonize with the bark of trees and the like on which they have to sleep exposed to the light. Protective colouration was much talked about at one time, although no one dared to suggest that anything other than Darwinian evolution was responsible for it. But, if this idea was correct, then why are there so many varieties of brown moths each with an intricate and often beautiful pattern? One generalized pattern

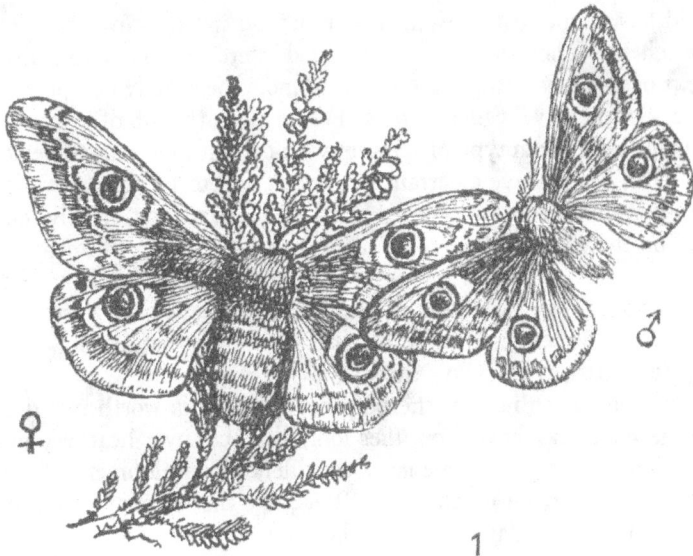

Figure 14 False eyes on insects. 1. Emperor moth, *Saturnia pavonia*, Mardon, Devon. Female pearly grey, male reddish brown, male has antennae like radar scanners to find female on heather moors. 2. Peacock butterfly, *Vanessa io*.

would have done just as well. Mutations did not improve the camouflage scheme. They simply gave an added interest to the moth collector. The process of evolution here seems to me to be exactly comparable to the task of the naval cadet who used to be given the job of working out the plans for a given type of warship with certain functions to perform. The moth has to have a certain food plant and to be able to escape as far as possible the attentions of birds when it is resting. Surely too the 'eyes' on the wings of the emperor moth or the peacock butterfly could only have been designed by a mind not so very different from that of man himself (fig. 14). How could they possibly have been produced by trial and error of chance mutation? It is no wonder that Adam Sedgwick laughed at part of Darwin's theory.

While on the subject of the emperor moth, it is worth mentioning that the male, as I have seen, flies long distances over heathery moors to the female. Only the male has a considerable development of comblike projections from its antennae. This, like that of certain beetles, is clearly a form of radar built in to the insects.

Protective 'eyes' are not confined to insects. They are also found on fish and birds. The butterfly blenny is not widely known, but the John Dory, *Zeus faber*, must often have been seen on a fishmonger's slab (fig. 3.1). It is, in fact, one of the more delicious food fishes. However people are frequently put off buying it by its grotesque and formidable appearance. It must be infuriating to fishermen to know that shoppers will not buy some of the better tasting local fish because they look ugly and instead prefer what they call 'iced muck' from Greenland or the White Sea. How many people for instance ever buy gurnards? When I used to catch and bring in gurnards as a boy, it took a lot of persuading before I could get them cooked. Yet they are splendid eating. I had an old fisherman at one time in my boat, who used to tear off their skins with the black stumps which were his teeth. This rather put one off one's breakfast; but it was nothing to what happened when he had had the fangs removed and been fitted with false ones. These were evidently uncomfortable and ever afterwards one had to be careful in sitting down on the coach roof of the boat. Here one might easily have been bitten by two sets of dentures, looking as big and forbidding as the teeth of rocking-horses. I do not think he ever used them for eating and only put them in when he went ashore. This he preferred to do when we were at anchor riding out a gale of wind. He would wait till it was blowing its hardest and then make some excuse for going to get something. One watched the old man and the plunging dinghy with misgiving and I am certain he only did it to make sure that I had a rope's end handy for him when he came back. Of course I was always on deck waiting for him when he did return. He was a wonderful boatman, but without a rope's end handy he might easily have capsized, or been blow out to sea.

This rapid survey of what the pendulum seems to be trying to say about the relationships of colours in the animal world brings me to what I think is a most important matter, the significance of the numbers of the rates themselves in relation to other rates. The numbers of course simply tell us what length of cord will send out a vibration which will bounce back off a particular thought pattern, whether it be the mental idea of a certain metal, or an entirely abstract idea like memory or anger. The rates are simply measurements of length. But they represent a certain speed of vibration and there is reason for thinking that these vibrations occur as very high sound waves. We might think quite reasonably of the rates as notes. If this idea is correct, then a metal gives off a single note and a compound a chord composed of as many different notes as there are elements in its composition. I find that the easiest way to represent such compounds is by a series of concentric circles with their radii, which have been shown to be of the same length as their rates, in measured proportion.

Now with anything of this sort one naturally begins by arranging one's rates in a vertical table, but I soon realized that all rates were confined between the figures of 0 and 40 inches (I shall drop the word inches from now). I also noticed that groups of important ideas all fell at the quarter points. That is to say they all fell at the quarter points of a circular diagram of 40 divisions, and that the cardinal points of North, East, South and West corresponded to 40, 10, 20 and 30. This was so remarkable that I found it hard to believe. Here was most dramatic evidence of the existence of a master plan behind the rates. Some mind must have planned this. It could not possibly have happened by chance. Furthermore had I not been working in inches and had been using the fashionable scale of centimetres, it is most unlikely that I would ever have noticed the symmetry. But the inch is a natural measurement derived from the human thumb, which the centimetre is not. What I was looking at was a perfectly natural plan derived from a perfectly natural set of measurements. I think the evidence derived from the rates is such that it implies a creative mind working in much the same way that the human mind works. Anyone who can use a pendulum can find all this out for himself and see that I am telling the truth. But if the facts support this inference, a matter in which I feel I am really scarcely qualified to judge, then it is quite clear that some mind beyond any possibility of chance has always been at work creating and thinking out new forms. I say mind, but looking as widely as possible over the range of living forms and at the remarkable life cycles which have been discovered amongst them, I seem to see ample evidence of the operation of not one mind, but many. It all has the appearance of delegated authority. When one considers, for instance, the life story of such parasites as the well-known liver fluke, which begins the cycle as a small snail on damp meadow grass, is eaten by a sheep and finally changes into a sole-shaped organism feeding on the sheep's liver, or that of ichneumon wasps, which lay their eggs on caterpillars to hatch out and eat the caterpillars alive, we seem to get a glimpse of an entirely different type of mentality at work from the one which designs the innocuous beauty of a brilliant butterfly. At the risk of upsetting conventional religious beliefs, which I have no wish to do, I think the evidence of this earth, and of the universe as a whole, all points to a hierarchy of creators working under one, far greater mind. I do not think, either, that the stage of mental development attained by what we might call the sub-contractors is so very much higher than that reached by mankind itself. Whereas the mentality of the master mind is infinite, that of the creator of the liver fluke has the appearance of being strictly limited, and itself one in a series of inventors to whom the mechanics of evolution has been entrusted. It is the manner in which this evolutionary process may have been carried out which we have to investigate next.

Eight

When carrying out our experiments it has become clear that there is a universal range of rates peculiar to each and every thought form. It is evident that a compound has more than one rate and a living organism a number of them. It is also evident that a living organism, besides giving off the separate rates of the compounds of which it is composed, has also a stronger master rate of the species to which it belongs. This is evident from the way in which insects react to the master rate of their food, which we have discussed already. All this can be examined by any competent operator and can be to some extent measured. It is as much science as the measurement of a voltage or the distance away of a star. But it seems to be a science on another plane. We have already seen in the case of Cretaceous sea-urchins that the rates appear to last for an indefinite time, and we shall see presently that they do not seem to be confined to the laws of earth distance. Although this may be a worry, or even seem impossible to scientists whose thoughts are restricted to the Victorian concept of a three-dimensional world, these ideas are already on the way out. Physicists are no longer able to distinguish between energy and matter, and zoologists have begun to realize that telepathy is a power to be reckoned with in the study of evolution.

Quite soon in our investigations we discovered that man could detach a part of himself, of his mind in fact, and this detached portion would show as a rate from an object to which it had become attached. The sex of a painter of a picture could be identified as a rate coming from that picture. This was very easily tested. However it is noteworthy that it will not work correctly with a pencil drawing, for graphite, for some unknown reason, reverses the sex rate in the same manner that lead interrupts the rate completely. But, as long as a picture is painted, you can find the sex of the painter correctly without trouble. I have been asked to find the sex of a picture which I thought was clearly the work of a man. However the pendulum gave a female rate—it had been painted by the owner's mother.

This is a well-known phenomenon in the study of extra-sensory perception. It is known as psychometry and has recently been demonstrated in dramatic form in a book called *Psychic*, about a gifted Dutchman named Hurkos. But our pendulum psychometry is at once rudimentary and scientific. We find a given quality on a given and measured rate. It was clearly necessary to take the investigation further.

We found that many objects lost in antiquity and newly dug up responded to both the sex rate and the thought rate (27) of the person who had made or used them. This ranged from an Elizabethan blacksmith's iron work, to Bronze Age flint implements. It was necessary, however, to get some more definite information than this and I cast about for some suitable subject for experiments.

Now in the Early Iron Age, somewhere about 200 B.C. the sling became popular in war. It is a reasonably accurate weapon with an extreme range of about 200 yards. In all but the more wealthy communities the missiles, sling-bolts, shot, or bullets, were simply rounded pebbles of which the most suitable size for war weighed about 3 oz. Outside many Iron Age camps sling stones are very numerous indeed and from the variety of sizes it is clear that children were taught at a very early age to practise with a sling from the ramparts. I had picked up about 2,000 outside an Iron Age Camp at Wandlebury near Cambridge and I now proceeded to examine a sample of these. Most of the stones were quartzites, well rounded, water-worn stones, which had been brought from some distance to the hill-top on which the camp had been constructed. I meant to take a sample of 100 stones, but accidentally counted 110. I examined this sample carefully with the pendulum, for three rates, male or female sex (24 or 29) thought (27) and anger (40), which has the same rate as death. I felt that if the anger rate showed on the pendulum, the pebble had probably been used in war. It is a tedious and exhausting business to perform so large an examination, because you evidently use some of your own current in making the pendulum work. The result of this experiment was most interesting. Nine stones out of 110 gave no reaction for any of the three rates. They were also the most irregular. No doubt they were not sling bolts at all. All the others reacted to the male rate and none to the female. Seven stones reacted to the rate for anger. These were all larger than the bulk of the material and ranged in weight from 3 to 6 ozs.

The Iron Age camp on Pilsdon Pen in Dorset was being excavated at this time. Many sling stones were found inside it and many also on the slopes outside. I tested a number of each. All responded to male sex and thought, while large numbers inside gave the anger rate. I conclude that they had been shot into the fort in time of war. Many sling stones were found when Blackbury Camp near here was excavated some years ago. Most were found round the entrance gate. I could not find many lying on the surface, but the only one I did find near the rampart had the anger rate.

Now whatever way you look at this it is a most remarkable business. These sling stones were certainly not slung away after the Roman Conquest. Therefore the rates we got from them have been there for approximately 2,000 years. Something that men's minds added to the stones had endured all that time.

The point then arose, could we do this also? There seemed to be an easy way to test this. The sling stones from Pilsdon and Blackbury had all been collected and brought inland from the pebble beaches around this coast. Most of them are extremely well rounded ovals of flint or chert. It was decided to collect a sample of untouched pebbles from a local beach and see whether we could implant any rates on them.

My wife and I each collected 100 pebbles from Seaton beach. We used a pair of tongs to pick them up and drop them into a bucket. On our return we tested them and found no rate except that for silica (14). I held one in my hand for half an hour. It then responded to the thought rate, but not sex. Then I threw a few and tested them again. They then reacted to both thought and sex.

We then carried out our experiment. My wife threw 50 pebbles and I tested them. All gave the 29 rate for female sex and 27 for thought. I then threw 50 and she tested them. All gave 24 for male and 27 for thought. Finally I threw 50 and tested them myself with the same result. We were unable to induce the rate for anger.

Now it is obvious that this experiment could be repeated *ad nauseam*. Somebody might like to do it. It would be quite unnecessary. A friend has indeed tried experimenting with weapons in museums and found the anger rate to be quite common. Obviously you can induce these rates on inanimate objects and this goes a long way to show that psychometry is not a product of anyone's imagination. We have demonstrated that something from the human mind can be induced on what I call the 'field' of an inanimate object. The sensitive, or medium, holds an object belonging to a given person and then proceeds to relate what he or she appreciates concerning the owner of that object, as perceived in tiny pictures. I have seen this done on many occasions by different sensitives and it is very impressive. However it cannot be controlled. What is seen and told is a matter of chance. What is told by the pendulum is the answer to exact and definite questions. Did a man or a woman handle this object? Were they angry at the time? No doubt the range of questions could be very much extended and it would not be very difficult to make up a kind of 'Identikit' picture of the maker or owner of an object. I have enough rates to try this now. But few objects would give simple answers, for many people may have handled them. In spite of this drawback, sensitives have considerable success with handwriting, and the manner in which Hurkos assisted the continental police in dealing with criminals was quite astonishing. His sensitivity, following an injury to his head, must be more or less unique. Nevertheless we can demonstrate that this is not a bogus subject, but one which can be placed under scientific control.

Some thirty-three years ago I spent the best part of a year in making experiments with a sensitive, with the idea that if there was anything in it (which many of us doubted), it might be of value in the study of archaeology. At the time I came to the conclusion that much of what the sensitive saw, as she described it (she appeared to see scenes in tiny pictures), came from my own mind. I published this opinion in *Ghost and Ghoul*, saying that each object was only a link between the sensitive's mind and that of the experimenter. Nothing I thought, and I still think reasonably on the evidence then available, was locked up in the field of the object. We have now shown that this idea was wrong. It is necessary to look at psychometry in quite a different way. I will give an example of one of the sensitive's object readings: At the entrance of Loch Kentra in Moidart, to the southward of the entrance, is a sandy bay backed by dunes. On the ordnance map it is called Cul na Croise, but the real local name is Traig a raevagh, 'the rover's strand', and there are stories of desperate battles there. Be this as it may, in the bare places between the dunes one used to be able to pick up medieval objects, iron arrow-heads, clinch nails from boats, glass beads and other trivialities. Others found good medieval brooches and coins. The place is spoilt now, for it was used for commando training in the Second World War and is so littered with bomb splinters, cartridge clips and so on that it is impossible to distinguish the older objects among them. It is a pity because, as well as the medieval objects, there was an Early Bronze Age land surface in the dunes from which came fragments of beaker pottery, flint arrow-heads, minute scrapers and barbs of that period. Anyway, in the summer of 1934, I visited the Rover's Strand and returned with a small medieval brass brooch. It was an unimportant and common object, like a little curtain ring, about an inch across, with a wire pin which ran round it on a loop. These are usually regarded as thirteenth to fourteenth century. I put this directly in a box and later handed it to the sensitive without touching it more than could be helped. She held it, looking at it in a dreamy way, and then told the following story. She saw, that is she appreciated in tiny pictures, a large upper room in what she thought must be a castle. In this room a very fierce looking old woman was sitting. Standing facing her was a dark girl in a brown dress. She was wearing the brooch. There was also a tall fair young man in the room. There was a serious quarrel taking place because the girl wanted to marry the young man and the old woman was opposing this. There was also a large fierce bird on an upright perch. 'Could this be a falcon?' the sensitive asked.

The historical and archaeological background is this. Three miles away, on a tidal islet at the head of Loch Moidart, stands the ruined Clan Ranald castle of Tioram. It is little more than a square keep with not much sign of a bailey wall. The castle is thought to have been built by a warrior chieftainness, Amie MacRuari, an ally of Edward I in his Scottish wars, but it stands on a much older site, which has produced the remains of a fifth to sixth century bronze hanging bowl of the type known to many people from the Sutton Hoo ship.

Now, as far as it goes, the whole thing could be correct. The room could have been the hall in Castle Tioram. The old woman may have been Amie MacRuari. The little brooch was of approximately the right date. The girl could well have been wearing a brown dress, for tweed dyed brown with crotal lichen is the commonest colour to be employed in the west. The sensitive had no knowledge of medieval matters and had not seen Castle Tioram.

There were very many similar readings and I have taken this one at random. But it is clear that, to be of any value from an archaeological point of view, you would need less of the personal side and much more small detail. An object would have to be picked up with a pair of forceps, or tongs, so that nothing passed from the excavator into its field and so on. But all this could be done under controlled supervision and so much digging is now done that it would be well worth serious consideration.

One point is worth noting. Not only did the sensitive see a tiny motion picture, she also heard what was being said. On another occasion, I picked an iron medieval arrow-head out of the rubbish outside the foundations of a small house in the sand dunes at Hogh bay in Coll. This was handled as little as possible and given to the sensitive. She described and drew a picture (she had been to the Slade), of a bareheaded man sitting cross-legged on the ground and holding the arrow-head. He was apparently making it and at the same time he was singing a sort of work song over and over again. The sensitive tried for a long time to get the words written down on paper. They were clearly in Gaelic, a language which she did not know, but what she wrote down was:

Niach, niach shald relachan
Lucha, lucha vor an lahin

This appears to have no meaning as it stands and is probably incorrect.

I have spent some time on these reportings because some points are evident and important. Obviously a sensitive does not see these things with his eyes, neither does he hear with his ears. These are mental pictures and sounds. Ordinarily one would assume that they are the products of imagination on the part of the sensitive. But a study of a number of such reports shows that this cannot be the case, because among the pictures which might or might not have been the imagination's efforts to reproduce antiquity, are others which can be identified as coming directly from the memory of the investigator. When reasonable care has been taken to pass an object on unhandled to the sensitive, no memory pictures appear to pass with it from the investigator.

We have seen too that abstract ideas, such as thought, can certainly be induced on the fields of inanimate objects. It seems, therefore, that a whole range of such ideas would be induced at the same time, including sound rates as well as pictures. If this reasoning is correct, then somebody whose mental outfit was correctly tuned in would act in the same manner as the pendulum, but on a far more elaborate scale. It is difficult for me, whose university training ended in 1923, to get a reasoned mental picture of all this. Nothing in one's studies suggested that humanity might be fitted with a sixth sense, which could appreciate matters outside time and distance. In fact such an idea was blasphemy. But what has taken me thirty years to grasp would be understood in as many minutes by modern children, who are brought up on television to be shipmates with ideas like dematerialization. I have noticed that children catch on to the idea of the pendulum at once. But then two generations ago the children of Southleigh and other villages to the north of us beyond the hills used to look for hidden metal objects with pendulums made of cotton reels on threads, and their mothers used to find the sex of eggs with a needle suspended from a length of cotton. The sex of an unborn baby was determined over much of the country by using a wedding ring, in a similar manner, over the mother's stomach. Telepathy was widely known and future or past events determined. But science, rigidly tied to a world of five senses, would not even accept the practical use of the divining rod; although professional diviners went round locating water for well-sinkers. It was a curious blind patch, in its way quite as blind as some of the less probable religious dogmas. It was the very opposite of the scientific outlook, which is in duty bound to examine everything. Here were things, known from remote antiquity by most of the population to have some foundation in fact, simply ignored because no scientist dared show an interest in them for fear of being regarded as crazy. It never seemed to occur to the mass of the intelligentsia that there might be something missing from their original terms of reference. If there are six senses instead of only five, then clearly very much which is still regarded as fundamental to learning has to be rethought. Of course the trouble was also due to impressions based on faulty knowledge of the Old Testament, in particular verses in Leviticus and Deuteronomy warning the early Hebrew against the practice of divination and such-like black arts. It knew nothing of anthropology and did not realize that the authors of the Koran also were up against the problem of primitive worship and witch doctors, not unlike the voodoo ceremonies of today. One of the rituals of which the bible authors complained, 'passing through the fire', is the fertility rite of jumping over bonfires which is scarcely extinct in this country today.

I hope I have said enough to show that psychometry must be regarded as something which really does take place and is as much factual as the existence of hypnosis, which now takes a recognized place in the medical curriculum. But beyond this we can say that there is a practical side to it. Just as the rates of sex, anger or thought can be found in the fields of sling stones used 2,000 years ago, so much can be interpreted by the pendulum from the blood, handwriting or former possessions of another person. Distance and time do not come into it. I know that this seems completely absurd to very many people. They have just not been conditioned to think in this way. I did not believe it myself until a great many tests convinced me, and I see no reason why what I now write should carry conviction either. Still, almost anyone can test it for himself, and if he cannot make it work the pendulum tells us the reason, or one of the reasons. It ought to work for everybody if he is completely fit, although some undoubtedly have more power than others, and some have about the same potential as cats.

Now if you take a letter from an unknown person written in ink (pencil will give some faulty answers) and test it with the pendulum, it is easy to find whether it comes from a man or a woman. You can also find if the writer is in good or bad health. If the pendulum says that the writer's health is not good, you can easily work out a table of rates for the different parts of the body and find out what is wrong with him. I am not going to give a list of these rates here for two reasons:

(1) I am by no means certain that they could not be used to cause harm by some ill-disposed person.

(2) There seems to be a considerable risk of what one might call rebound, from the patient to the operator.

People whose nerves are shown to be bad cause great exhaustion to the operator. In fact we now test the nerve rate first and, if it has a bad reading, have no more to do with it.

Having given these two warnings, I will say that we would be only too pleased to give our list of rates to any qualified medical man or chemist. Over a couple of years we have watched several human guinea pigs twice daily. One was a particularly good case (we had never met him and the only link was a piece of handwriting), because he left this country, flew to Australia, visited Tasmania and returned by way of the United States. We knew neither the times nor the destinations. Now when this guinea pig set out there were certain small readings for ill health. You obtain the readings by noting the number of revolutions the pendulum makes. After a certain number of turns on the rate for a particular illness, it returns to an oscillation. The number of turns for a serious illness may be well over a hundred, but for a slight ailment it will only be a few turns. Our guinea pig evidently reached Australia in safety. We knew that much. Once there the warmth after a dull wet winter in England evidently had a good effect for the number of turns on the pendulum fell to almost nothing for all rates. This was splendid. The holiday was doing the guinea pig good.

Then one day we observed a marked upward jump in the number of gyrations. Of course we were recording all readings, dates, hours, etc. The rates jumped up on a given day at a given time. They crept down again slowly after that, but never reached the low level they had been at before. We did not learn the probable cause for a week or more. Then we were told that the guinea pig had gone to Hobart in Tasmania the day after the disastrous bush fire, which was reported in this country. This visit corresponded within a few hours with the upward turn in the readings. We assumed that the smoke and general feeling of depression in Hobart had caused these phenomena.

We continued our recordings, having no idea where the guinea pig was. After some days there was a second upward jump and similar readings from organs not previously affected. We deduced some kind of gastric infection. Again it was over a week before we learned what had happened. The guinea pig had been returning to England and had stopped at Chicago. There he had picked up an intestinal infection, which was known as the 'Chicago bug'. As before, the times corresponded very neatly. But they do not always do so. Another guinea pig who we were recording fell off a chair on to some rubble when doing some building work. The pendulum showed a very marked upward jump in the readings three hours before the accident happened. This was not overseas where some clock variation had to be taken into account. It was fifteen miles from here.

The first case, besides showing the apparent capabilities of the pendulum in the matter of diagnosis, also demonstrated the point that, unlike other subjects such as electricity where the power fades in accordance with the square of the distance, the rays from the pendulum are outside ordinary measurement. Distance makes no difference. The second case shows the same to be true of time.

This is not the first suggestion we have had about time, by any means. The sling stones had been used two thousand years before and still retained the rates induced by man. The fossil sea-urchins had sex rates which covered an infinitely longer period, running into hundreds of millions of years. But this is the first case in which time is in the wrong order. The pendulum reading showed the accident before it had happened. This is completely impossible according to three-dimensional science.

To understand at all what is happening, it is necessary to take another look at what has been learnt about the rates. I have mentioned already how they can all be plotted on a circular diagram of 40 divisions. On this circular card north (40) is at the top together with death, cold, anger, sleep, black and so on. South is at the bottom with east, red, on its right (10) and west, green (30) on its left. Round the circumference of the circle all the other rates lie according to their numbers. Some, such as the rate for psychic ability, which I call the psi rate ($9\frac{1}{2}$) are fractional. Copper is $30\frac{1}{2}$, with blue and cobalt, and mercury $12\frac{1}{4}$. There are so many names now that I cannot construct a complete diagram which would print clearly. There is one in my last book, *A Step in the Dark*, but even that is not very clear. Therefore I have been content with diagrams illustrating various groups of ideas (fig. 15).

Now several ancient religions appear to have hit on something resembling this circular plan. Someone, a long time ago, did a lot of work and knew a lot about this subject. In the lore of druids, alchemists, gnostics, witches and so on, as well as in our own folklore, there are signs that once a great deal had been discovered. And in the teaching of the Buddhists of Tibet great stress is laid on 'the wheel of life', and on the 'four quarters and ten directions'. The Tibetans have of course studied this subject with great thoroughness in their own way. While we try to approach it along the path of science, their method is entirely mental and their aids are not instruments but contemplation. It is interesting then to see that they place seven colours in the

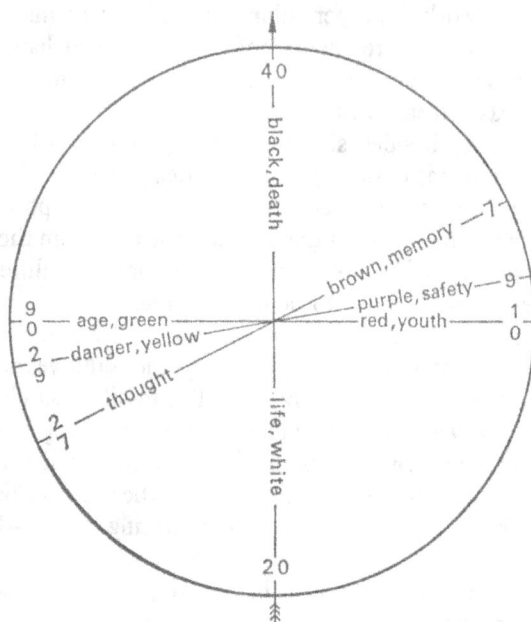

Figure 15 Relationships with colours. Rates in inches. I have not included north, south, east and west in this diagram, but of course north is at the top and is true, not magnetic, north.

halo of Buddha. Excluding black, white and grey, which are hardly colours, we have the rates for seven as well: brown (7), purple (9), red (10), yellow (29), green (30) and blue (30½). These are not the primary colours of the artist, who believes green to be a compound of yellow and blue, but are primary colours in nature. Orange makes seven.

Now it is possible to arrange all these rates in another way. You can take your circle arranged in spokes, and mark the length of each rate up from the hub along its appropriate line. The resulting picture is an Archimedean spiral ending at 40. Each dot, which, when joined to the others next to it, forms part of the spiral, is in reality the central point of the base of a double cone at right angles to the plane of the original circle. The circumference of the base of the cones cuts the point at which the observer stands. Since the points 40, 10, 20 and 30 can be shown to be orientated to the true as opposed to the magnetic points of the compass, it is clear that the rays from even the smallest objects proceed outwards at right angles to the surface of the earth. But a far more important point is apparent. The spiral cannot possibly end dead at 40. The spiral must go on, and this is what the Buddhists believe

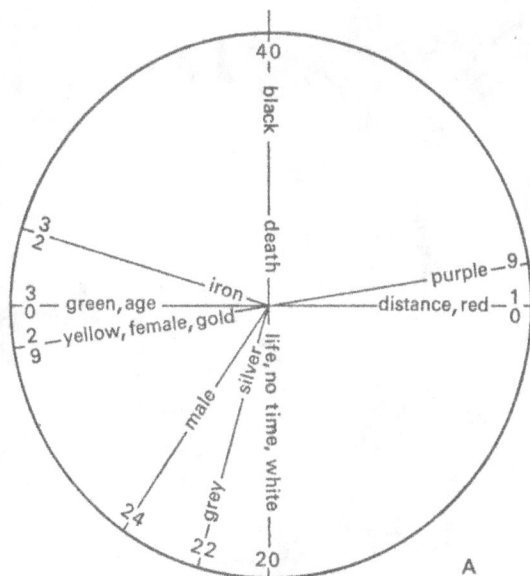

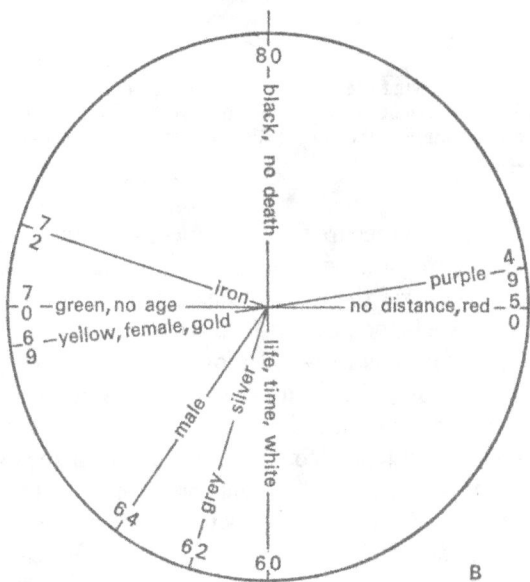

Figure 16 Diagram of examples of rates, in inches, from two levels on the spiral. A is the normal 'earth' level and has no rate for time because this is moving away and affords no obstruction to rays sent from the pendulum. Time appears to be static in B, the next level. There is no 'death age' nor 'distance' in B; but colours and metals are as in A. Sex persists in B.

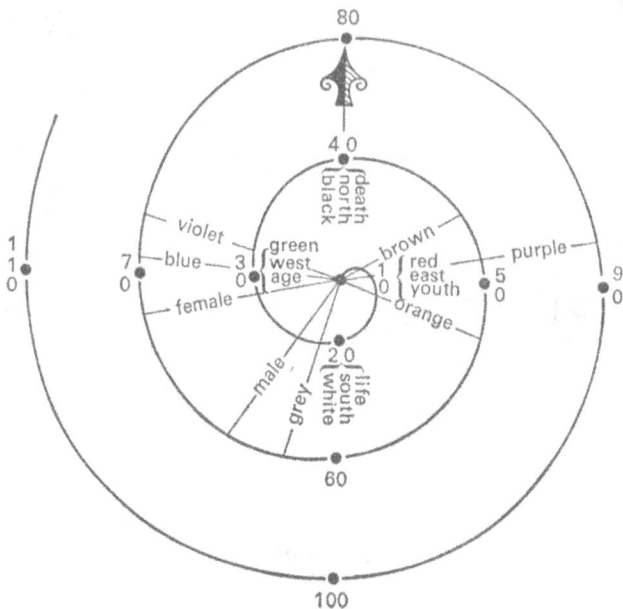

Figure 17 Diagram showing the spiral track on which the rates lie. Only a few are shown. The great extent of the spiral can easily be demonstrated by taking the figures from the table at the end of the book measuring them on to a forty divisional circle.

and teach. Their wheel recurs for ever unless you can get free from it.

It is quite easy to show with the pendulum that our spiral of rates also continues. It passes the point of death at 40 and repeats the rates exactly as they were before, but with 40 added to their number. Purple is thus 9 + 40, or male is 24 + 40. However there is one great difference. The central point of each double cone has shifted. You can thus place a material object on the floor and find the circle around it. The object is there for you to see, touch or smell. But there is also a mock position for that object and round that position you can find a circle with the original rate and a new rate with 40 added to it (fig. 16). You cannot perceive the object in its second position by any of the five senses. However you can find it there with the pendulum. It exists in another plane. The whole range of mental ideas exist in another plane beyond the rate for death. But there are exceptions and they have a bearing on what we have been talking about (fig. 17).

You cannot find a rate for time on the first whorl of the spiral. This is presumably because time is always passing here and you cannot

94

pin it down with the pendulum. On the second whorl, beyond the rate for death, you can find a rate for time. It appears to be static, although this is beyond our comprehension. It is the same as the second whorl's rate for life, 20 + 40. In other words, if you happen to pass the point of death and are living on the second whorl, it takes no time to do anything you want to do. If that is so, anyone engaged in creating a species has only to draw up his design and he can then put it through all its evolutionary stages at once.

There is a third whorl outside number two. It is rather a trouble to investigate, for its rates are those of the first whorl plus 40 and again 40. This makes a very long cord on the pendulum, which is difficult to measure and awkward to use. I use the well of the staircase for experiments. As far as I have investigated, number three is again a replica of number one; but on it there is once more no rate for time. Events are evidently once more in time sequence as they are on the first whorl. There for the moment I must leave it, for I have nowhere suitable to look for a fourth whorl. It seems most probable that there is one and that what we have been examining is a measured demonstration of the truth of the Buddhist belief in the endless repetition of life and everything else. If so however there seems to be something left out in what is reported about their belief, for I have never heard of timeless intervals between the lives.

Of course I may have reasoned incorrectly from the information at my disposal. I do not trust my powers of reasoning. But others must experiment and see that the facts are there as I have told, for this appears to be something of vital importance.

Nine

The object of this book is not really metaphysical. We are only trying to find a plausible explanation of how the tremendous display of variety in the living world may have been produced. Now I think we should go back over what has been written in the last 35,000 words and see where we stand before adding a little more information for consideration.

We began by taking the current belief in the Darwinian evolutionary theory and the survival of the fittest. This we examined critically and, taking examples from most of the great orders, found numerous cases which did not appear to fit in at all with Darwin's original idea. We came down in fact on the side of Professor Adam Sedgwick, who once advised Darwin not to publish his ideas as much of it was ludicrous and the rest liable to cause great harm to mankind.

In Part Two we have been looking at results obtained from the study of some branches of parapsychology, a subject which is still widely known as 'the occult'. This is perhaps not a bad name, for 'occult' means hidden and it is all as dark and twisty as a path through a hazel wood on a moonless night. Using the immemorial aids to divination, the hazel fork and the pendulum, we found that it was indeed possible to locate and dig up completely hidden objects from beneath growing turf. This was done by finding the characteristic ray for given metals and other chemical substances. The ray was known by the length of cord on the pendulum, which was termed its rate.

It was then found that rates could be found for many things other than material objects. Colours, points of the compass and many abstract ideas all had rates. Next it was observed that some of these rates for abstract ideas could be found attached to material objects. The sex of an artist, artisan or flint worker, all could be obtained from the objects they had made or used. The investigation was extended to cover such things as thought and anger. Rates for sex, thought and sometimes anger were all obtained from sling stones discovered from both inside and outside Iron Age camps of two thousand years ago. This coupled with the discovery that sex rates could be obtained from fossil sea urchins well over a hundred million years old, suggested that the endurance of some kinds of thought form was probably without limit in time.

We then experimented with the artificial induction of thought and sex rates into the fields of untouched beach pebbles and found that this could be done without difficulty. Here we had a practical demonstration of what is known to the parapsychologist as psychometry. By finding the rates for many parts of the human body and employing pendulum psychometry, it was shown that with the use of letters, or blood spots, it was possible to diagnose some illnesses and accidents at a very great distance. In fact it was possible to keep a check on the health of a patient as far away as Australia.

Then we turned our attention to the distribution on paper of the rates themselves. Here we appeared not only to find evidence for the existence of a master plan, but also for that of at least two more planes of existence for the human mind after the point indicated by the pendulum as being that of bodily death.

This is such an unusual story that at every stage we have found it most hard to believe and have been forced to go back to the beginning and look at the evidence for what the pendulum could produce from beneath the surface of the ground. After reviewing this each time we could only say, 'Well, it undoubtedly tells the truth in these seemingly impossible circumstances, so it may be assumed to be telling the truth again when it tells us other impossibilities'. We are making no attempt to prove anything. If we did so it would simply mean wasting a great deal of time which can be better spent in widening the range of the investigation and trying to establish the general picture. There are many people who seem to like making huge numbers of tests in order to try to prove some point or other. We can leave this kind of thing to them.

Now at many points in the preceding chapters the point arose that it would be far easier to account for the development of this or that living creature by the assumption that some external mind designed it, than by any reliance on evolution through stray mutations giving it a better chance in a hypothetical struggle for existence. Our experiments with the pendulum took us much further than that. They seemed to show beyond reasonable doubt that there was a master plan behind everything which had hitherto been ascribed to chance. If we read the story aright this plan went so far as to place warning colours on poisonous, or dangerous, plants, fish, insects and mammals, while at the same time it painted others with the colour sign of safety. Here we will branch off again once more and see whether we can form any idea of how the ideas of an external mind might work.

There are other ways of using the pendulum to the one we employ by using rates. The most popular is that of using a short cord of roughly 6 inches long. Most operators use this method in conjunction with a very large number of samples of what they want to look for, whether it be traces of tuberculosis or a golden treasure. The principle is that the pendulum will swing backwards and forwards between two things of like kind, two nickel pennies, or two lumps of alabaster, and will gyrate when the two specimens are of different materials. With sexes, however, this is reversed. The pendulum gyrates between two males and oscillates between a male and a female.

We have found a number of practical uses for the short pendulum. It will say at once what foods or drinks are good for you, by oscillating when you swing it between you and something good and the reverse when it is harmful. There is no difficulty in picking out the poisonous alimentary canal of a lobster or the dangerous parts of a crab. Pills which do not suit you cause an immediate gyration. But it has none of the advantages of being adaptable to accurate measurement of the other method and, although I have tried it for the apparently most improbable art of finding things from maps, I have not done much of this and have never been able to check up to see whether it told the truth.

For instance I have experimented to see what it might say about several missing treasures. The most interesting is the celebrated Armada silver supposed to lie at the bottom of Tobermory harbour in the island of Mull. So much money has been spent over the years in looking for this treasure that I wondered whether there was really anything there to be found. The pendulum gave a very slight reaction for silver over the spot in the harbour where an Armada ship is known to lie. It was so slight that it hardly seemed to indicate any great mass of silver. The ship lies in deep water, I believe 18 fathoms, 108 ft, almost exactly where I have sketched the anchored destroyer in fig. 18. The galleon would not have been half the length of the destroyer. The hull of the wreck is much silted up. Years ago I lay at anchor close by and watched a suction dredger working fruitlessly on it.

Long ago too, nearly fifty years now, I listened to the traditional story of the loss of this ship being told in my late uncle's house of Glenforsa on Mull. As I remember it, it went as follows: In the autumn of 1588 the defeated Spanish Armada was forced to return to Spain round the north of Scotland. One galleon, short of food and water as they all were, put into Tobermory. There the chief of Maclean Lachlan Mor, from Duart castle at the other end of the Sound of Mull (fig. 19) made a bargain with the Spaniards. He would victual the ship

Figure 18 Tobermory harbour. The destroyer is at anchor where the Armada ship blew up. Sketched 25 September, 1949.

if they would assist him in storming the castle of Mingary on Ardnamurchan, which belonged to their enemies the MacIains, a sept of the MacDonalds. The Spaniards agreed to this, but they did not trust the Maclean and insisted on his leaving a relative as a hostage in the ship.

The Spaniards and Macleans duly stormed Mingary castle and the little bay where they landed is still known on the maps as Port nan Spainteach, the Spaniard's landing. This part of the story is presumably true.

However the Maclean did not produce the promised stores. Instead, the hostage managed to fire a powder train and blew up the ship. A feeling of gloom seems to hang over Tobermory to this day.

Now verification that something had happened came from the report of a spy in English pay at the Scottish court. He said that destitute Spaniards had arrived on the mainland from a galleon whose name was not that of any known Armada ship, but was assumed to have been *Florida*, a garbled form of the name *Florencia*. This was one of the finest ships in the Armada and spoken of by the English as the *Florentine*, although her real name was the *San Francesca*. She was a new galleon of 50 brass guns and had been commandeered from the Grand Duke of Tuscany in the most high-handed manner. She was hotly engaged

Figure 19 Sketch map to show Armada treasure problem. 1. Tobermory wreck. 2. Rudha an Ridire wreck. 3. Duart castle. 4. Mingary castle. 5. Spaniards' landing, Port an spainteach. 6. Traditional site of buried hoard of silver, Creag an Airgid, 'the silver crag,'

several times in the Armada's passage up the Channel and was no doubt considerably shot about.

The story goes that she carried a quarter of the pay of the Duke of Parma's troops waiting in the Netherlands to be transported for the invasion of England. Whether this is true I do not know, but the belief in it has led to all these searches for the treasure, which was claimed as an hereditary right by the Dukes of Argyll, former Admirals of Scotland.

When many years ago at Duart I had the pleasure of listening to the late chief of Maclean, Sir Fitzroy, telling stories of the Crimean war, there were several iron guns lying outside the castle. These were small breech loaders, known as 'man killers', as opposed to the big muzzle loading guns which were 'ship breakers' (fig. 20). They were spoken of as coming from the Tobermory galleon. I doubt this. The Tobermory ship lies in deep water. The guns were of the right type for that date, but there is another ship from which they probably came. This wreck is traditionally said to have been the *St John the Baptist* and to have stranded on Rudha an Ridire quite close to Duart castle on the opposite

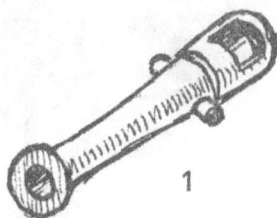

Figure 20 1. Breech-loading brass gun of the type known as 'man-killers'.
2. Brass muzzle-loading culverins, known, in Elizabethan times as 'ship-breakers'.
This is a detail from a Sèvres vase. The men are fitting a new bush to the worn
touch-hole of the gun.

side of the Sound. I think the guns came from her. I tried the pendulum
over Rudha an Ridire on the map. There there were strong reactions to
both silver and gold.

Now whatever the vessel is which lies at the bottom of Tobermory
harbour, it is not the *Florencia*. There are two reasons for saying this.
First, a piece of silver plate was recovered from the vessel with the
arms on it of a Spaniard who is known to have been aboard a different
ship. Second the *Florencia* is apparently known to have returned to
Spain in a battered condition. It is not known what ship lies shattered
in the Tobermory mud. There would be more hope of success for skin
divers working off Rudha an Ridire.

But why were the Macleans and Spaniards so set on destroying Mingary castle? Of course you can assume hereditary enmity between the
Macleans and MacIains. However I will be bold enough to make another

Figure 21 Halzephron cliff, Gunwalloe. This cliff is the tombstone of three treasure ships wrecked there on different occasions. The name apparently means 'Hell's cliff'.

suggestion. A couple of miles inland from Mingary is a hill known as Creag an Airgid, 'the silver crag'. This has a tradition of a buried silver treasure on it. It seems possible to me that what really happened was this. When the second galleon came ashore on Rudha an Ridire, the MacIains got to it first and managed to loot a haul of silver from the wreck. This they took back to Mingary and hastily carried up into the hills for concealment. At the very least they might expect to rouse the wrath of the Duke of Argyll and bring the Campbells down on them. They were MacDonalds themselves and everyone knows what that means. But the Macleans learnt that they had been thwarted of a rich prize. They went to the Spanish ship lying in Tobermory and told a story of disgraceful theft. From the Spaniards' point of view the expedition was to recover the money which was the only pay they were likely to see. In the subsequent storming of Mingary, no MacIain survived who knew where the treasure had been buried. It was known to be in the area of silver crag and no more. There are caves somewhere on the silver crag, for a stream running close to it is called the burn of the cave of the pigs. It would be worth a good investigation of this area. Even if it is not the Spanish treasure it would be worth a search. The

Figure 22 Rhossilly bay, Gower. 29 May, 1946. One of Catherine of Braganza's dower ships is thought to lie at extreme low tide in this bay. The wreck in the foreground is a local coaster.

pendulum over the map indicates silver on Creag an Airgid, but, as I have said before, I have as yet no faith in this.

I like these mystery stories of the sea. In 1922 I found a little midden on the west of the isthmus on the Shiant Islands in the Minch. In it were two squared bronze nails from a Roman ship. Some shipwrecked men had used broken planking from a vessel to make a fire for boiling limpets. What ship was this sailing in waters which Rome, in theory, scarcely knew? It could have been one of the ships stolen by Agricola's mutinous German mercenaries, some of whom are known to have sailed right round Scotland and ended up as slaves in Holland. Or what story lies behind the gold bars fished up by men years ago on the west of Barra in the Outer Hebrides?

Then there is the disaster of the dower fleet of Catherine of Braganza when she married Charles II. Three ships sailed and only one arrived. One came ashore under the terrible cliffs at Gunwalloe in Cornwall. She drove so far under these cliffs (fig. 21) that the bulk of the dower money has never been recovered. But some has. Fishermen and miners fought for it on Gunwalloe beach in the moonlight. One Portuguese silver coin is still in the keeping of the vicar, as he told me. A second

103

vessel was stranded on the great sandy beach of Rhossilly in Gower (fig. 22). When the sand shifts from time to time at very low tide, men have been lucky enough to stumble on her bones and hastily grab what silver coins they could before the sea covered it all again. One local squire is said to have driven his coach on to the beach and filled it. But there is a more sinister side to the story. Round the headland to the north of the bay a small hoard of contemporary gold coins was once found in a cleft of the rocks. Some Portuguese officer from the ship had probably been robbed and knocked on the head, like the well known case of Sir Cloudsley Shovell, who was wrecked in the Scilly Isles. He was apparently washed ashore alive, but was murdered and had his fingers cut off by a local woman for the rings that were on them. The Rhossilly thief could not remember in which crack he had hidden the gold.

We, however, used the short pendulum for quite another purpose, and that was in an experiment to attempt to demonstrate pendulum telepathy. I described this in some detail in a former book, *Ghost and Divining Rod*. Telepathy, a branch of parapsychology, is almost universally accepted now and has in fact, as I said earlier, been suggested as a factor in evolution. However, we wished to see if we could demonstrate it in connection with the rates.

For this purpose we chose the sex rates as something which could easily be recognized. I had a considerable number of one species of fossil sea-urchin for I always pick one up when I happen to see it. I figured some of these for a detailed account of our experiment in *Ghost and Divining Rod*. They are heart-shaped casts of the interiors of the shells. There is a considerable difference in size and pattern between those which react to the male rate and those which the pendulum designates as female. For the other part of this experiment we took two sterilized bottles containing some male and female hair respectively. When a bottle of male hair is placed opposite a male fossil and the short pendulum is swung between, there is opposition as I mentioned before. The pendulum gyrates because the ray is turned back on itself. If, however, you repeat the performance with a bottle of male hair and a female sea-urchin the pendulum oscillates backwards and forwards. The ray passes uninterrupted between the two. If you substitute female hair for male, of course you get the reverse result.

Now what we wanted to find out was whether if one operator swung the short pendulum between two specimens in one place, a second operator in a different room could tell what result was being obtained by the first. The second operator, who could neither see nor hear the first, was to use a long pendulum tuned in to either the male or the female rate of the sample of hair taken to be used against a fossil by the first operator. There was nothing but a slate floor under the long pendulum and a concrete floor beneath the short one. The two rooms were on different floor levels and there was a thick stone wall between. Nothing could be seen or heard between the two rooms. The long pendulum was entirely on its own, and its operator did not point in the supposed direction of the short one. Everything was as secure as we could make it and it seemed evident that if the second operator obtained correct results on the long pendulum the information was being conveyed by mechanical telepathy. Watches were synchronized, and at given times the first operator swung the short pendulum between two fossils while the second operator, in ignorance of what sex of fossil was being tested in the other room, swung the long pendulum. We found that which ever of us operated which pendulum, the long one always gave the correct answer to the sex of the fossil being tested. You could change the operators about, change the sex of the hair and the rate on the long pendulum and change the sex of the fossil. It could not deceive the pendulum.

Of course, to prove this, the experiment ought to be performed hundreds of times. A warning is, however, necessary here. All pendulum work entails the use of some current from the operator's body to project the ray through the pendulum. As far as our work goes, we find that a great deal of current is in fact used up and the operator soon becomes tired. After testing for sex and thought rates in 110 sling stones, I was very tired. I think that it is most probable that, if you did more than a couple of dozen of these telepathic experiments at one time, the operators would become tired and errors would start to creep in. I do not know and the number is a guess. However I think that this would happen.

Probably the way to test whether the operators are becoming tired is by using the psi rate of $9\frac{1}{2}$. This I regard as a measure of potential. As I said earlier, you measure it by counting the number of turns made before the pendulum ceases to gyrate. We have tested 84 people for their psi rates. This can be found from their handwriting just as well as by reading direct from the actual person.

Fifty-four persons had what we may perhaps speak of as psi potentials of varying values. They range from 0 to at least 50, but they are not constant. They go up and down according to the person's bodily condition. During bronchitis, one guinea pig's potential dropped from a normal of about 45 to 30, and remained there till the illness was over. People with a potential of 15 and upwards can usually work the pendulum quite well. The only professional medium whose writing we were able to test was no higher than 18, whereas we had about a dozen of 45 or over. From around 30 and upwards people seem liable to have more extra-temporal and other unusual experiences than most of their neighbours.

There remains more than a third of the selected group who have no reading on 9½. Instead they have one on the opposite side of the circle at 29½, which we are calling minus psi. It is seldom very large, and when small fluctuates to the positive side and becomes 9½. When we tested the few minus psi persons who had a reading of 30 or over, we found that they were in poor health according to what the pendulum reported. This showed as rather bad readings for the nervous system in particular. There were generally traces of something else wrong as well. By no means all persons with bad nervous readings have minus psi potential, but it is something which is worth bearing in mind.

Animals have psi readings and such cats as have been tested mostly have a potential of about 45, as high as any human in fact. Dogs we have not yet tried.

It seems evident that a psi potential is really a necessary part of the human make-up, but in many cases it is becoming weak, or converted into something else. Since examining nervous cases with the pendulum is intensely exhausting, it seems probable that the minus psi draws current from plus psi and these people become, in a sense, vampires. Many readers must have experienced a feeling of exhaustion after being in close company with another person. This is, I think, due to the leakage from plus to minus psi. It flows from the highest to the lowest and those persons whose psi is normally under about 10 probably never experience this phenomenon at all. With much practice in pendulum work your normal psi rate appears to rise, but this does not warrant too much use of the instrument at any one time. This leads to exhaustion. Should one suspect that another person is draining power from you, it can be checked to some extent by being outside the range of the rates, that is 40 + 40 inches.

Although psi is in many ways similar to electro-magnetism, it is by no means the same. For one thing, we have seen that it does not diminish with the square of the distance. For another, it can pass up from the three dimensional earth plane into a second and third. Psi is not bounded by time, or distance, as we know them. As I have suggested in another book, it may well be the same force as that which operates gravity. It also appears to be related to ultra-sonic sound. This is the force which has to be considered when thinking about both telepathy and psychometry.

Of course you cannot have one without the other. Telepathy has to be used by the psychometrist to extract impressions from an object in such a way that they may be comprehensible to the mind. We usually think of telepathy as being the process where a single idea appears to arrive almost simultaneously in the minds of two people. This seems to be a chance happening and it is often difficult to establish which mind originated the thought. But telepathy is much wider than this and in the case of animals it is clear that individuals of differing species can carry on conversations by its means. In the case of birds, whole flocks operate as one, wheeling and diving with no word of command. Telepathy, in fact, is an alternative method to speech as a means of communication, and can be quite deliberate.

I said that the psychometrist must make use of telepathy and this may seem an inaccurate statement. But telepathy has to be the means by which the information stored in the field of an object can be transferred to the mind of the operator. The information may be pictorial, or in sound form, but whatever form it takes it cannot pass into the operator's mind by its own action. Telepathy provides the beam on which it passes. The beam can, as we have seen, be broken down into various rates and these we are beginning to appreciate, even if we do not know what they really are. But then does anybody honestly believe that he understands electricity? He may know all there is to know about harnessing the force, but what it really is remains an enigma.

It is the same with telepathy. We may know that it can transfer thought forms from one mind to another, or from one object to one mind. We may soon learn to control it in the manner that electricity is controlled. Yet it may never be possible to say what it really is, beyond the vague statement that it consists of high velocity vibrations.

There we will leave telepathy for the moment, having demonstrated, I hope, that it can be utilized mechanically in the manner that electricity can be so utilized. We can, moreover, note that we have now two branches of parapsychology, telepathy and psychometry, both of which seem capable of being studied in a normal scientific manner, but both of which are evidently outside the range of three-dimensional science.

Ten

What we have learnt so far is of considerable help in understanding some otherwise completely mysterious happenings. This is particularly true in the case of ghosts. Here let me make it quite clear that a ghost is not a spirit. It is a picture, a sound, or a feeling of horror or pleasure, which is not in its correct place in the sequence of events. Spirits are living persons whose normal dwelling place is not on the same plane as the one on which we are living. They do not concern us here.

My wife and I are both trained observers, but over a period of years we have only been certain that we have seen ghosts on very few occasions. I have told the stories in other books and will not repeat them here. We have heard ghosts even less frequently. But we have experienced feelings of horror often, and of pleasure, which was not our own, now and then. We have also smelt smells of cooking, tobacco smoking and such like, which were impossible under the circumstances in which they occurred.

The world is divided about equally into those who believe in ghosts and those who do not. But it is evident that many of the disbelievers would not be able to experience ghosts, in any case, because they have a minus psi rate. Others have some non-scientific and usually obstinate mental attitude which prevents them making full use of their powers of reasoning. For most of them see ghosts and hear ghostly noises without observing it. The image on a television screen is a ghost and so is broadcast sound. The only distinction is that one is an accidental and entirely mental product, while the other, although still mental in origin, is the end product of an elaborate series of mechanical devices. They are ghosts because they are not in their true position in the sequence of time and they are also in their wrong position in space.

A great many ghosts must be experienced and not recognized as such because there is nothing about them to suggest to the observer that they are in the wrong place in time. On other occasions the observer is either not thinking about the matter at all, or else is not a good enough observer to pick on essential details. But, although surveys have shown that about 20 per cent of the population has at one time or another experienced something not in the correct time sequence, the happenings cannot in any case be very common. Still, they are a natural phenomenon and can be examined objectively. You might just as well say that aurora borealis does not exist, because you have never happened to see it, as to deny the existence of ghosts.

I am not going to say anything about poltergeists here because they do not concern the phenomena we have so far studied in this book. But we have had a little experience of them and not long ago I was asked to try and stop one such series of unpleasant happenings. I apparently succeeded, although I had very little idea how to set about it.

The visual ghosts which my wife and I have experienced and which could be demonstrated to have been out of their correct time position fall into three categories. They were human, animal and mechanical. The last sounds absurd, but was actually an ancient car seen by my wife on a straight stretch of road. It turned off the road when it had approached within about 50 yards of our own bonnet and went through a hedge, either by way of a gate, which was shut at the time, or over a considerable ditch. Then it vanished. Two similar cases have been described on Westward Television in the last few months. In all three cases, the ghost cars not only vanished, but were of old-fashioned types. Sitting beside my wife in our car I saw nothing of the ghost. It could, I think, only have been seen from along a fixed narrow track on the road, that is, only when sitting in the driving seat of a car moving towards the ghost. These ghost cars seem to be on the increase now, which is scarcely surprising. The reader should note that obviously a car cannot produce a picture of itself, neither is it a spirit. It is the type of car and its performance which is always noted and not the driver or passengers. It seems clear then that it must have been a former viewer who produced a particular scene and that only when on the beam of that viewer's line of sight can the picture be seen. It is out of its proper time context, otherwise it is a perfectly rational picture of what must have been recorded in that viewer's mind. There is no reason to assume that some serious accident once occurred in relation to the ghost car. As we saw with our pebble experiments, thought rates can be implanted in the fields of inanimate objects with little difficulty and can later be located with the pendulum. In these cases of car ghosts all that need be assumed from them is that some viewer once noted their appearance and behaviour with sufficient intensity to fix the rays composing the picture in something inanimate.

From a study of these ghosts it becomes clear that certain localities are more suitable for pictures to be fixed there than others. In a former book I attempted to classify these for convenience in writing about them. I called them by the names of nymphs of classical antiquity, a dryad field for one in a woodland place, a naiad field for one by a stream, an oread for one in rocks or hills tops and a nereid for the sea. The Greeks and Romans noted the occurrence of non-human visitors in such places and, not knowing as much as we are now beginning to learn, assumed that they were supernatural beings. But they were wrong. All they were seeing were mental pictures produced by someone else at some other time. The place where my wife saw her ghost car has a dryad field in the form of a copse on either side of the road.

On 22 February 1959 I saw a ghost just down the slope from the house here, which I have described in *Ghost and Ghoul*, and also on television. It was that of a woman who has been identified by somebody who knew her from a drawing I made from memory after the occurrence. She appeared in broad daylight on a sunny morning beside another woman who was really there. They were at the end of the house some 60 yards away from, and below me. We saw the second woman within a few moments of the sighting and asked who her companion was. She assured us that there had been no other woman, still less one dressed in clothes a generation out of date. The details of her clothes were so clear to me that I could identify a wreath of white roses round her hat. There is a photograph in existence showing a similar female figure, with a similar hat but different dress, on the other side of the house. It was given to us some months later. Here we have a very definite and detailed picture of someone none of us had ever seen, but who was recognizable to those who had known her, appearing for no apparent reason and completely out of the time sequence. Once again there was a suitable field, in this case a dryad field, for the reception of the picture. A very small stream ran at my feet. Since the woman can hardly have known what she looked like when gazing up at the hill above, we can conclude that her picture was fixed in the dryad field by someone unknown who saw her from the point where I was standing.

It should be noted that it never struck me that I was seeing anything remarkable and I would never have known that I had seen a ghost had I not asked her companion who she was. Then it was at once clear that there had been no companion at the time. Only then too did it occur to me that her whole outfit was uniformly grey and she had no colour about her, whereas our friend was dressed in vivid tartans and blues. This ghost is unlikely ever to be seen again, for a new kitchen has been built over the spot on which she stood.

The third type of ghost was seen by my wife in the Branscombe village hall at a jumble sale or some equally mundane performance. A woman came into the hall with a little, nondescript brown dog on a lead. As there was a second dog already in the hall, my wife feared there might be a dog-fight and the incident was impressed on her memory. The woman passed out of sight further down the hall, and my wife became occupied with other matters. Presently the woman went out again with no dog on a lead. Later this struck my wife as strange. Where was the dog? There was no dog. Inquiries showed that the woman had had a dog answering my wife's description of it. She had been very fond of it, but it had been dead five years. There was another important point. The woman at that time lived in a house on the other side of the cliff from the village and the dog was never allowed to leave the cliff. Here some other person must have apparently added the picture of the dog to that of the woman when she noticed her at the hall.

We have had something similar to this in which the ghost was alive and talking to us. I have described it in *A Step in the Dark*, but I will do it again because it is so interesting. About three years ago we were for an hour or so having coffee with, and talking to, a couple we did not often see. As I have been trained to report to my wife on the turn-out of any women I happen to talk to when she is not there, I noted this woman's outfit. In fact I thought it was rather smart for the occasion. She had on what I would call a 'silk' dress of a light chocolate colour and an openwork gold brooch with a yellow stone in the centre. I wondered if this was a cairngorm.

In the car on her way home my wife remarked on how the woman had aged and stressed the whiteness of her hair and the white sweater she was wearing with an imitation Celtic silver brooch on it. I had noticed the hair, which to me appeared only slightly dusted with grey.

Now we are both careful observers and trained to remember what we have seen. For instance, although there is only a tiny patch of sea visible from this house, if I notice a warship passing five miles out and have time to snatch the glasses and look at her for the few minutes she is in sight, I can then sit down and draw a silhouette, which can be identified by a sailor who knows our modern ships. I have had the actual vessel, and not just the class, recognized and named. This may be something of a trick, but it is still fairly good observation. I do all my water-colour painting from memory, although I do make a pencil sketch in the field.

My wife has much the same kind of observation and memory. I was standing beside her once as she steered us into the narrow, rock-encumbered entrance to South Rona harbour. I said quietly to her, 'Now, there is a rock you can't see there on your port-hand not 50 yards away.' We passed that safely. 'And there is another over there on your starboard bow', indicating it with my hand. 'And there is a third just there'. Nothing more was said. We sailed on up to the head of the harbour and let go behind a sheltering island. A year later, after having been into many holes and corners in the meantime, we came to South Rona again. As we came into the entrance I said, 'You know your way in?' 'Oh yes', she answered. 'There's a rock there and there and there.' Not many men could do that, even professional fishermen. She had never been to South Rona before that first time. I have never seen her take out colour patterns to match in the shops; she takes the tints she wants in her memory.

You can say then that we are reliable observers, yet we had apparently seen the same woman in two completely different kinds of garment, and of different colours. Her ornament was of different metals and her hair of different shades. One of us, and I think it must have been me, had been seeing her as a ghost. But that ghost was alive, well and talking. She is alive today.

I think the answer must be that it was the husband who made me see her as she used to be some years before. He was so fond of her that he always projected an image on to her of how he liked to see her. This I think I received telepathically in my mind all the time we were there and it was stronger than the true picture which my eyes reported to my brain and so to the mind.

All these ghost pictures are really carried directly into the mind without the use of sight. They do not come into the three-dimensional world at all, but belong to another where time does not pass. You can call them fourth-dimensional or extra-dimensional or what you will, but they are psychometrical projections transferred to the mind by telepathy. If we knew enough rates, or could be bothered to spend the necessary time, we could make an identikit picture of a ghost by swinging a pendulum in its particular dryad, naiad, or whatever field it is that holds it.

As far as our experience goes we have never felt any form of emotion where picture ghosts are concerned. This is to be expected if, as I have suggested, they are just scenes projected by some onlooker. The only case in which emotion is likely to be felt is when the onlooker is horrified or very delighted by what he saw. It is quite a different matter with the purely sensory type of ghost, which I call a ghoul, for this is evidently projected by the mind of somebody who is personally involved.

A typical ghoul is a horrible feeling of depression or fear accompanied by that of considerable chill. These ghouls are not rare at all and they vary very much in intensity. They agree with visual ghosts in that they become stabilized in dryad, or naiad, fields or even in the stone work and walls of buildings. They also agree in being displaced in the time scale.

I have described our most unpleasant local ghoul in two books already and shall only mention it very briefly here. It was, and probably still is, located at the little naiad fields of streamlets, and in the rocks around Ladram Bay. It is usually felt in warm, muggy weather, which evidently aids its transmission into the observer's own field, his psyche field as I call it. At least a dozen people of our acquaintance have made contact with this ghoul over a period of several years in advance of the time of the event, which evidently caused it. But quite the most unpleasant occurred to my wife two years before this happened. She was standing on the cliff, noticing the feeling of depression, when something said in her mind, 'Wouldn't you like to jump off?'

In point of fact, someone, whose name we will not repeat, did jump off the cliff near where she heard this and the body was recovered from the sea near Portland Bill. He left some of his gear at the spot. He had evidently taken some time in deciding to do it, and had walked from the car park above Sidmouth. In his terrible state of mind he projected his misery into the rocks and streams all round Ladram Bay. But the point is that these were clearly put into those fields in the same way in which the Iron Age slinger put his thought and anger into the slingstones he used in battle. The feelings projected by the suicide were strong enough to need no pendulum to record them and they affected at least a dozen people, but the process was exactly the same. We know now how ghouls are produced. Thought forms become separated from the mind of the thinker and joined to the field of something else. Once this has been done, the thought forms leave this three-dimensional plane and are out of time succession. You cannot tell then whether the event which caused the separation of the thought forms from the parent mind has taken place already, or is to come. The Abbot of Downside told on television of a precisely similar ghoul which was felt before another suicide. My mother and I met another years ago, in a wood in Berkshire, very near to the time a third suicide took place. Here you have the dryad field of the wood taking the place of the naiad fields at Ladram.

It is worth noting that in no case did a picture of the suicide appear. There is no reason why it should. No one knows well enough what they themselves look like to be able to project a thought picture. Somebody else has to do this. Yet the person does have an idea of what his own voice sounds like, to him. It is not what it sounds like to others, as you can tell by listening to a sound recording of your own voice, but you think you know what you sound like and can project it. This is what my wife heard asking her to jump off the cliff.

Sound projections are reasonably common. I have heard bodiless steps passing my door late every night when staying in a Cambridgeshire farmhouse. This is a frequent phenomenon all over the world. Somebody has lived in fear of some other person's arrival. A feeling of cold accompanied the steps I heard. It is not so intense as that felt with the ghoul at Ladram. I think it is due to a sudden loss of psi current on the part of the observer and is comparable to the tiredness caused by operating the pendulum.

There is another kind of visible picture, which is of an entirely different kind and does not really concern us here. All Buddhists and Hindus believe that they have a double. The same story is told by those who study these matters in the West. People are said to be able to leave one body resting or asleep and travel where they will with the other. We have some evidence that this is correct. Anyway, if you see such a double, it is not a ghost. I have once seen what I take to have been a double, but it was not human. The story is worth telling. On Friday 28 October 1966 I was rung up by a woman I did not know, who asked if she might drive down from the home counties and consult me about some matter or other. I agreed to the suggestion, and rather to my surprise an interview was fixed for 11 a.m. on the following Monday. On Saturday my wife's old cat was found to have a broken tooth and poisoned mouth. An appointment was made with the vet at Axminster for 11.30 a.m. also on that Monday morning.

At about five minutes to eleven on the Monday morning my wife started out in the car up the hill at the back of Hole with the cat in his travelling basket. It is twelve miles that way to Axminster. On the top of the hill she met another car in the lane, bringing the visitor to see me. It arrived here almost exactly at eleven o'clock.

I greeted the visitor, who was being driven by her sister, and brought them both into the hall. This is a real Tudor hall with a Henry VIII doorway, but it is not open to the roof, as someone has put a second floor above it. Its axis is approximately east and west with a big open fire at the west end and a chimney so large that you can look straight up it to the sky. Somewhat unexpectedly the fire burns extremely well and I had lit it to welcome the visitors. In front of the fire is a big fire stool, which you can sit on, and on the north side and close to the fire, a sofa. Opposite this, on the other side of the fire, are two armchairs, one beneath the south window and the other at an angle facing the fire end of the sofa. The rest of the hall is open with a few chairs, tables and chests in it. It does not get cold as you might expect, the walls being 3 ft thick.

I put the woman who wanted to see me in the corner of the sofa nearest to the fire, and her sister near her. I myself sat, not in the chair under the window, but in the other so that she would not get the light in her eyes when talking to me.

We had just begun to talk, and the time must have been about seven minutes past eleven, when she said 'Is this the cat you write about in your books?' I looked up and saw what was unmistakably my wife's cat standing with all four feet on the fire stool and apparently smelling the visitor's hand, which was almost touching his nose. 'Yes', I said, 'that is our cat, but he's getting very old now'. In point of fact he was over eighteen. Then I thought no more about the cat, and was involved in a conversation I had to think about. I never saw him go, although I have a feeling he did jump down off the fire stool and walk away to the corner where his drinking bowl was kept. I did not think again about the incident for over a week. It seemed perfectly normal at the time. Presently the visitors left, and afterwards my wife returned having left the cat with the vet to have the tooth out under an anaesthetic. She told me that she had had to sing to it all the way to Axminster to stop it yowling. It was half Siamese.

The cat never got over the anaesthetic and poisoning and in ten days it was dead. We were very distressed for it was a very wise animal and skilled at making its wishes known by telepathy. Still it had had a wonderful life, and like Nimrod was 'a mighty hunter before the Lord', although I rather drew the line when it brought in live adders.

After the cat's death I suddenly remembered the incident with the visitor and realized that it was an impossibility in a three-dimensional world. All the time the cat was standing on the fire stool, it had also been in a basket on the road to Axminster. It was a twelve mile journey and my wife was only just in time for the appointment with the vet at 11.30 a.m.

I wrote and checked up with the visitor, who confirmed that the conversation had taken place, but said that neither she nor her sister had seen the cat. How the conversation could have taken place unless she had seen it, I do not know!

I cannot explain this happening in terms of ghosts and rates. Neither, since the conversation was confirmed, do I think that it was possible for me to have imagined it. The only explanation seems to be that cats do have doubles, and that he had projected his double to his home in preference to being shut up in a basket. If this is the correct answer, then the cat is still alive on another plane. Curiously enough, this explanation has been accepted without hesitation by some Roman Catholic priests. I do not think that in the East it would cause any comment at all. They know that this kind of thing is quite natural.

Actually, the cat had a psi potential of 45, which would be very high for a human. It had been observed to exercise a kind of radar to learn about happenings 450 yards away on the other side of a stone wall 2 ft thick, and it knew where any of its friends were when they were quite out of sight. I think it had really performed this trick with its double on many occasions, for it was frequently found on the far side of shut doors where it seemed impossible for it to have appeared. In fact, for years it was spoken of as a key-hole cat!

Eleven

This chapter differs from the earlier ones in being largely concerned with our recent experiments in extra-sensory perception, and in theories about this faculty. I must make it quite clear that life is far too short for me to spend the time which would be necessary to obtain proofs of what the experiments appear to show. Others can follow up what we have begun. Here I can only tell of what the evidence seems to indicate, and then pass on to some other clue. My object is to find a framework which can eventually be filled in.

I have already talked about the pendulum rates, that is the length of cord between the bob and the windlass, and how it has been found that a given rate is characteristic of a given conception, whether this be material or mental. I have mentioned also the gyration of the pendulum, which is an indication that the correct rate has been obtained. However, there is a second measurement, which can be used to distinguish concepts on the same rate. This is found by counting the number of revolutions which the pendulum makes before it returns again to a backwards and forwards movement. If, for instance, we take the rate of 22 inches, we find that lead, silver, calcium and sodium all respond to it. However if we count the number of revolutions we find that lead makes 18, silver 22, sodium 30 and calcium 35 turns. In fact each metal has two co-ordinates and this applies, apparently, to all concepts.

Of course, it is obvious that these co-ordinates can only be part of a much larger scheme of classification which remains to be discovered. There must be a whole series of numbers in front of the 22, which we have as yet no means of discovering, and it is known that after the pendulum has taken up an oscillation again it will presently begin to rotate in the opposite direction. This it presumably another co-ordinate, but we do not yet know what it indicates. With the two that we do know, however, we seem to be able to learn some remarkable things, and the experiments I am now going to talk about were made in order to explore this line.

It was noticed that some insects had the same pendulum rates as the substances on which they fed. Stag beetles had a rate of 11 and this was the same as that of oak. Dung beetles all had a rate of 16 and so had dung. But here our second series of numbers, the revolutions, seemed worth investigating. The case of the dung beetles, the scarabs, was obviously interesting. I shall not write down 'rate' and 'revolutions' each time, for this is unnecessary. I will just give the figure for 'rate' first, and separate it from that for the 'revolutions' by a colon. Dung, cow dung in this case, is expressed then by the figure 16:36. To my surprise, the co-ordinates for all the scarab beetles I tried, several different species of *Geotrupes*, *Onthophagus* and *Aphodius*, were the same. Grass, the essential original constituent of the dung, was 16:18. This obviously indicated something of considerable importance in the study of zoology. I tried to extend the inquiry.

I have already mentioned the genus *Chrysomela*, which is a plant-feeding one. Since it appears to make no difference to the pendulum whether an insect is alive or dead, I looked up the old collections I had made as a boy at school. I found I still had ten species of *Chrysomela*, and two of these had specific names, which suggested the plants on which they fed. One was *Chrysomela menthrasti* and the other *Chrysomela hyperici*. This indicated that the first fed on *Mentha* (mint) and the second on *hypericum*, which is St John's wort.

I tried *Chrysomela menthrasti* first. The pendulum said it was 12:22. I went out to the garden and picked a sprig of mint. This also was 12:22. *Mentha* is one of the large family of labiates. Many plants of this order are useful herbs, and well-known to most people; lavender, rosemary, sage, thyme, balm, skull-cap, marjoram and so on all have their uses. It struck me as possible that other species of *Chrysomela* might be tied in some way to various members of the labiate family. As far as I know, the food plants of beetles have not been studied to the same extent as those of moths and butterflies. I had no means at hand of learning what a particular beetle fed on. Therefore I tried the pendulum over all my available species of *Chrysomela*, and tabulated the results. Each one had a rate of 12, except *hyperici*. This, to my surprise, at the time, had one of 13.

Although it was now late in the autumn, I was able to find three species of *Hypericum* in the garden. They all also had a rate of 13. Since all my other *Chrysomelae* had a rate of 12, and one labiate, mint, had this also, I collected all the species of labiates I could find and tested them. The table opposite shows the result.

This is a remarkable table. It was compiled so late in the year that many plants were withered and gone. It seems probable that in summer it would be possible to find plants with counts to fit *Chrysomelae graminis* and *marginalis*, although they are

Beetle's Name	Rate	No. of Revolutions	Plant's Name
	12	9	Rosmarinus (Rosemary)
Chrysomela varians	12	12	Thymus (Thyme)
	12	13	Prunella (Self-heal)
	12	14	Salvia (Sage)
C. graminis	12	15	
	12	17	Stachys (Woundwort)
C. banksi	12	18	Lamium (Deadnettle)
C. marginalis	12	20	
C. menthrasti	12	22	Mentha (Mint)
	12	23	Melissa (Balm)
	12	24	Nepeta (Cat mint)
	12	26	Betonica (Betony)
C. polita	12	28	Scutellaria (Skull-cap)
C. haemoptera fastuosa	12	30	Glechoma (Ground Ivy)
	12	33	Origanam (Marjoram)
	12	35	Lavendula (Lavender)
C. goetingensis	12	36	Ajuga (Bugle)
C. hyperici	13	13	Hypericum (St. John's Wort)

(*C. fastuosa* and *C. goetingensis* are shown on fig. 4).

not common beetles and their food plants may not be common either.

Naturally I did not leave the investigation at this stage, and experimented with other plants and insects. A brilliant little green beetle, *Cryptocephalus aureolus*, is often found within the petals of the common yellow *Leontodon* (Hawkbit). They both responded to 14:28. *Donacia dentipes*, found in the vegetation near stagnant or slow-moving water, was 15:20, and so was *Juncus* (Rush). The well-known black and red cinnabar moth, with its black and yellow striped caterpillars, had the same rate and count as the Senechio plants of groundsel and ragwort on which it feeds ($21\frac{1}{2}$:12). The experiments could be carried on interminably, but there seems little need to do this, at the moment. There is good evidence that an insect is tied to its food by characteristic rates of vibration which the pendulum can detect (fig. 23.)

It is probable that this link between animal and vegetable is brought about at the caterpillar stage in the insect's life. It assimilates the food, which becomes part of its body and this retains the link when it

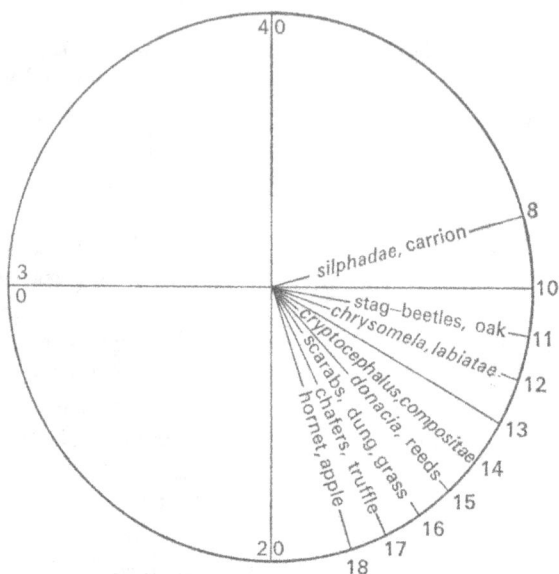

Figure 23 Relationship between some insects and their food. This could be greatly extended. Rates in inches. The number of pendulum revolutions indicates the particular species of plant or insect. See Figure 4. Both numbers are the same for plant and insect. e.g. *Cryptacephalus aureolus* 14:28. *Leontodon* (Hawkbit) 14:28.

develops through its metamorphoses into the perfect insect. Distances which seem little to us must be enormous to an animal less than the size of a green pea. How does it find its food? I think the answer is now clear. On its head it carries an instrument which acts like the water-diviner's twig, but in reverse. There are two antennae with a built-in response to the vibrations from the plant which its children have to eat. It is all perfectly simple and apparently most carefully thought out. This could never have taken place through any accidental evolution.

Of course no one with the slightest curiosity in his make-up can resist experimenting with the information freely presented to him by the writers of letters. We saw that something of the personality of an Iron Age slinger remained for two thousand years in the field of the stone he slung. It is just the same with a letter. Something of your personality remains in it, which is beyond what you said in the words you wrote on the paper. This is in accord with some modern theories of how memory functions, and although these have not yet been presented to the general seeker-after-truth, it seems evident to me that they must be nearer the correct answer than anything which has gone before. The holographic function of the mind is the coming idea.

What do you want to know about the people who have written to you? As this is, we hope, a scientific investigation, you want to catalogue them under various headings. We had over a hundred cards at Christmas and this seemed quite a big enough sample to learn something, although I might not believe what the pendulum said. Again and again I have to stress that I approach all this with complete disbelief. I am a most down-to-earth person and have had a scientific upbringing and training. I just do not accept anything the pendulum says without a struggle in my own mind. You must understand that we have worked out a table of rates, which comprises many things, and it seemed reasonable to try some of these in relation to others. I chose 9½ inches, which appears to represent the psychic potential of a person, and which I call the psi rate, 16 inches which apparently indicates the sex potential, 19½, which stands for blood and may show something about its character, and 30 inches, which stands for age. It soon became clear that the age rate had no effect on the sex or psi potential. Nevertheless this is the one I am going to discuss now.

In all, we tested 120 specimens, and whenever we knew a person's age the pendulum was right within two revolutions. The method was to start the pendulum gently swinging over the specimen of handwriting when it had been set at the 30 inches rate for age. Then, quite arbitrarily, but apparently correctly, we counted one year for each turn the pendulum made. It is not easy to be quite sure when the revolutions start and when they stop and this is why one is liable to an error of a year at either end. Critics of this method must try it out for themselves before they are in a position to form any judgement of its accuracy. It sounds complete nonsense and yet it appears to work. The proof of a pudding is not in what it looks like, but in how it tastes.

Now I am an archaeologist, and all archaeologists spend much of their working lives in trying to fix the age of things. Much of what you read in books and newspapers about these dates is complete guesswork. At the best it is the result of elaborate calculations of the possible resemblance between one thing and another. It is built up on the apex of an inverted pyramid, whose point is one object whose date appears to be reasonably fixed. The pyramid is always wobbling about and sometimes falls, disastrously. There is a method of analysis known as Carbon 14, but this is only of value for very ancient things and is known to be liable to considerable errror. It may be of some use for objects three thousand years old, but is useless for those of three hundred.

It seemed to me therefore that anything which only seemed to have

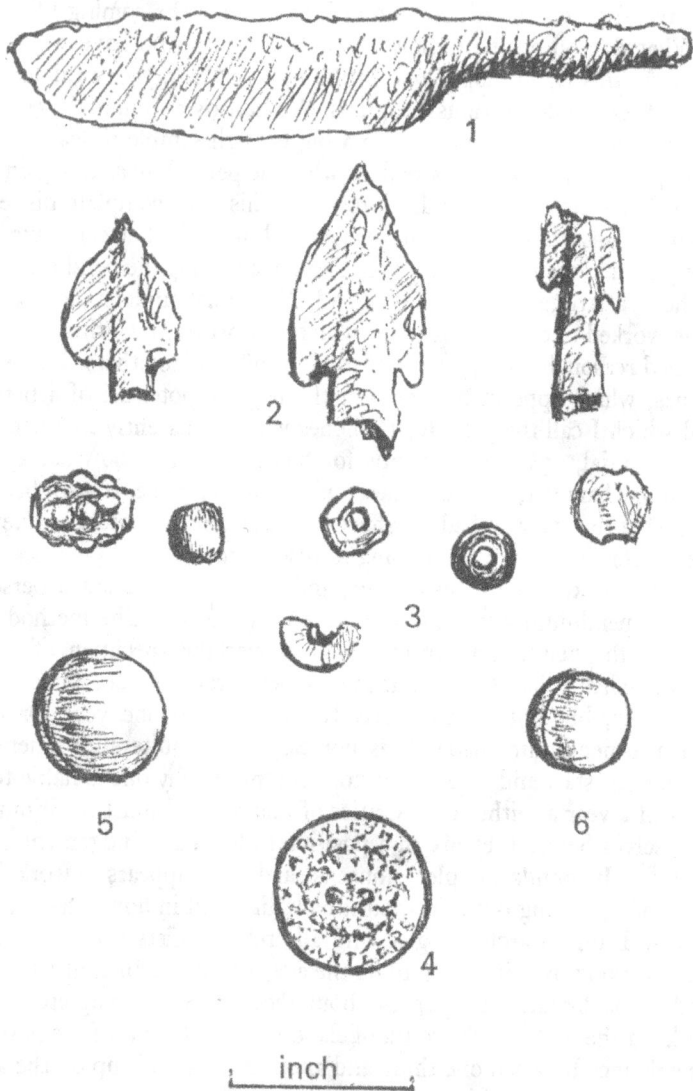

Figure 24 Objects from Cul na croise, Argyll. 1. Iron knife. 2. Three iron arrow-heads. 3. Six glass beads. 4. Brass button. 5. Lead musket ball. 6. Lead pistol ball.

a possible error of two years would be of vast importance to the archaeologist. Even if it could be shown to be right, I knew well that it would take at least twenty years for other archaeologists to believe it, for they will hardly believe that they have a nose on their face unless they are feeling it continually and seeing it in a looking-glass many times a day.

I tried out an experiment tentatively and in complete disbelief. I took a link lost from brass chain armour, which I had picked up long ago in the sand hills at Sanna bay on Ardnamurchan. I had always wanted to know its date and rather thought it was Roman, although it was larger than any Roman mail I knew. I put the link on the floor. Mail links are unmistakable because there is a tiny pin hammered through to fasten together the ends of each ring, a rivet. Then I set the pendulum at 30 inches. I swung it gently over the ring and it started to gyrate. I had greatly underestimated the tediousness of this process and how tired and mesmerized one would get. The wretched ball revolved eight hundred and twenty four times. I took the figure 824 from the year 1968 and arrived at a date of A.D. 1144. Yes, it could well be right. The object was not Roman, but belonged to what we would call the Norman Period in England, when mail of this kind was the normal armour of a man-at-arms. Sommerled, the ancestor of the MacDonalds, was King of the Isles at that time, and was frequently involved in fighting. The answer might be true, but I was not convinced.

Through the years I have picked up old coins from time to time in various places. I keep them in a box, each in an envelope, in case they may come in useful for reference purposes. I went to the box and took out one envelope. I did not know what was in it, but guessed from the size that it was either a bawbee of Charles II or a farthing of Henry III. I put the envelope on the floor, and went through the whole operation again. The pendulum made 642 revolutions, which gave a date of A.D. 1326. I took out the coin and examined it. It was a silver farthing of Edward I, or Edward II, whether it could be dated more closely I do not know, but the date of Edward II's murder was A.D. 1327. The pendulum was apparently just right and if I had miscalculated the number of turns by two, it was well inside the limit.

It is very tiring doing these long counts, but it would be perfectly simple to devise an instrument for recording the number of turns if it should prove worth it. Supposing it is right, what about finding the date of Stonehenge? Nobody really knows this, within hundreds of years. You could date any earthwork without digging it and then guessing the date from the lost objects you happened to find. I had to go on with this investigation. What I wanted was a run of objects of one group similar to the investigation of the ten species of *Chrysomela* beetle. As it happened, I had what I thought would do nicely.

In Moidart, on the north side of Ardnamurchan, there is a place called Cul na Croise, on Kentra bay. There are actually four little sandy bays, but only one concerns us. Above it is a wooded ridge known as Creaghan fitheach, 'the raven's crag'. One day in the autumn of 1924 I was in a boat off this bay, having with me a couple of cousins and one of the local Camerons. We had set a long-line for flounders, with perhaps a hundred hooks baited with lug worms, and were waiting for it to fish. The Cameron presently looked up and remarked that there had once been a battle in the sand-dunes ashore. At once I was interested, and asked when it had been. 'Ach, I don't know', he said. 'It was in the time of the Danes'.

Kentra bay is a lovely place, even now after the commandos were trained in landing there during the Second World War. A burn with little green flats beside it runs down from woods of scrubby trees to the dunes on the edge of the sea. Westward are the blue, jagged peaks of Rum and Eigg, and to northward the hills of Skye. This is a splendid place for beaching boats when the wind is off-shore and it is the best place for this purpose for many miles. It is not surprising therefore that local tradition tells of battles there.

However, local tradition is difficult to extract, and still more difficult to interpret. One heard of the 'Red Rover', whose name may have been something like Dewing, fighting on the beach and that its real name was 'traigh a raever'—meaning 'the rover's strand'. Whoever the Red Rover may have been I have never been able to discover. He is said to have been driven off, and to have died on an island near Dublin.

There was a tale of a second raid carried out by a dozen Irishmen, who were also driven off, chased to Skye, captured and their ship taken. But again no one knows who they might have been, and all that remains is the echo of a story of the bravery of a local weaver, a Cameron apparently.

My insatiable curiosity took me to the Rover's Strand on many occasions. Sometimes I walked for some miles through the woods from Acharacle on Loch Shiel, and sometimes I landed from a boat. I have hunted those wind-blown dunes till my back, bent from peering at the sand, ached so much that I had to give up the search. The sum total of my efforts was very small by archaeological standards, but it was also most intriguing. I found an early Bronze Age land-surface on which were scraps of 'Beaker' pottery and flint implements. Then I collected quite a number of glass beads, four black, three yellow, one blue and one white. I could not date them, although I have made a study of beads. There were fragments of at least ten barbed and socketed iron arrow-heads, and parts of four small iron knives, probably arm-pit knives. There were at least 100 iron clinch nails from a boat. All these iron objects and the beads might have belonged to 'the time of the Danes', for the Scottish crown did not obtain the islands till the thirteenth century, when it bought them for 4,000 crowns in 1266. There was a little brass ring-brooch, which perhaps belonged to this age too. But what was one to make of many lead musket and pistol balls, and a brass button embossed with a crown and the words 'Argyleshire Volunteers' (fig. 24)?

I decided that this was a fitting series on which to try the pendulum. If what it said made sense, then I would be prepared to accept its statements, with due caution, of course. I did not really know the date of a single object, except perhaps that of a little copper 'bawbee' of the reign of Charles II.

There were a lot of musket and pistol balls, but I had only kept two of the former and one of the latter. I tried these first. Remember, for it becomes more important in a moment, that I know I can be two years out in the counting. According to the pendulum, these balls were shot away and lost at the following dates:

Musket ball, A.D. 1785
Pistol ball, A.D. 1784
Musket ball, A.D. 1795

The button of the Argyleshire Volunteers was apparently lost in A.D. 1785. Now if the pendulum was telling something like the truth, it was obvious that no Red Rover, or boat-load of Irish pirates, had anything to do with this collection. The most probable solution appeared to be that the Volunteers had used the dunes for musket practice and one had lost a button off his uniform.

I knew nothing about the Volunteers. I had heard of the militia of course, and of the difficulties encountered by authority in enrolling them at the time of the Napoleonic Wars. I looked up what I could find.

It appears that Volunteers were a by-product of the Militia Act of 1757, and that by the next year officers were permitted to accept volunteers instead of compulsorily enrolled militia men. By 1778 there were Volunteer companies and corps formed independently of militia units. In 1783, with the political stupidity to which we are long accustomed in Britain, the Volunteers in England and Scotland were disbanded. They had to be hurriedly raised again on the outbreak of war with Revolutionary France, and in 1795 the invasion scare was in full swing. In 1798 the Volunteers were formed into 'armed associations' and the word 'Volunteer' was dropped. From this it is clear that the musket ball dated by the pendulum to 1795 is exactly right, and all the other three objects are within the two years margin of error due to the difficulty in deciding the exact moment at which the gyratory movement begins and stops. Perhaps the most impressive thing of all is that the gap of ten years during which the Volunteers were disbanded is reflected in the dates given by the pendulum. There are too few specimens of course, but my incredulity had received a knock.

Now ten arrows are not lost by accident, for anyone can see a 'clothyard' shaft sticking in the ground. These must have been shot away in action and never picked up again afterwards. We can infer then, that whoever shot them cannot have lived in the district, or they would have returned when all was quiet again to pick up what they had fired. Therefore I take it that these arrows had belonged to some force landing in the bay and that their landing had not been successful. Here we have some confirmation of the Red Rover tradition, but what was the date of the arrow-heads and were they all contemporary?

Through the years I have made a number of attempts to establish the dates of iron arrow-heads and have had little success. Although the name Red Rover suggested the Vikings, I was well aware that these arrows might have been of any date between perhaps the years A.D. 1000 and A.D. 1600. Bows were used by the English against the Spanish Armada in A.D. 1588, and probably much later in the Hebrides.

The tedious business of counting long runs of revolutions now began again. It was so tiring that I could never do more than two arrow-heads in one day. After a time, while watching the ball slowly swinging round, you begin to wonder if you are counting fifties or sixties. It is impossible to let your mind wander to anything else, and quite difficult to remember whether you are in the four hundreds or the five. You certainly cannot carry in your head the number of turns which had been made by the last specimen. It took twenty minutes to do each count.

The pendulum's answers for the date of loss, when the number of turns had been subtracted from the present year of 1968, were as follows:

126

A.D. 1340
    1344
    1341
    1344
    1342
    1341
    1343
    1341
    1344
    1343

Two knives, which I still have here, both gave readings of A.D. 1343.

It seemed clear, allowing for the possible error in some of the counts of two years, that an average shows that all these arrows could have been shot away, and the knives lost, in the year A.D. 1342. This ought to be the historical date of the Red Rover's abortive landing.

To anyone who had spent much of his life trying to fix dates by observing minute changes in the shape and ornament of objects, this result was fantastic. I was not sure that I liked it. If the pendulum was right, any child with a high psi count could be far better at estimating the date of an ancient object than the most learned professor of that particular subject. Still, one was trained as a scientist and so had a duty to record what one observed. However important an idea may seem to be to its originator, he must have the honesty to give it up when discovered facts show it to be wrong. Some well-known people today have prostituted their art by not obeying this principle. I may not like what the pendulum appears to be able to do, but I must accept what I find.

It was pain and grief for me to tackle the next stage. I had the nine glass beads from the Rover's Strand. I thought that they might have come from a necklace on one of the Rover's followers, but knew nothing about this particular class of bead; nobody else seems to know either. I was horrified and tired when I had tested the first one, a yellow glass bead with raised knobs on it (brambled, as it is called), because the count went to 970 turns, and this indicated a date of A.D. 998. I had eight others and each would take me about half an hour. During that half an hour you obviously use up a great deal of current and we do not know what this current is, nor how to recharge ourselves after it has been used. I was confronted with hours of strain and discomfort. At the end of it I would be faced with a column of dates, but I knew of nobody living who could say whether they were right or wrong. If they all varied considerably I should feel fairly sure that the dates were wrong. I have written thus far without knowing the answers and you can share my anticipation. Tomorrow, if all goes well, I hope to test the second bead.

This time, with a black bead, I counted 975 turns, which gives, as the date of its manufacture, A.D. 993. This was within five years of the date of the first yellow bead, a difference of about ½ per cent.

Before going on to measure the other seven beads, an idea came to me of how it might be possible to find out where they were made. It seemed probable that every country would have a pendulum rate and that the rate of the country of its origin would remain with the bead. I had no difficulty in finding that this was indeed the case. The rates were obtained by tuning the pendulum in over used stamps or letters from different countries. It is unnecessary to give many here. The ones which seemed most hopeful were Scotland 21½, Spain 11, France 21, Ireland 22½, Norway 23½, Denmark 19½, Germany 17, England 22, Netherlands 20. I had thought that the most probable countries from which the beads could have come were Ireland, where glass is known to have been made, or the great glass factories of the Rhineland. However, the pendulum gave a rate of 21 for the beads, which is that of France. Although I cannot prove that this is correct, I do remember having seen somewhat similar ancient Breton beads. I very much doubt, however, if Brittany is where they were actually made.

Before going back to the calculation of dates, I thought it would be interesting to learn what the pendulum had to say about the origins of other beads. Very great numbers are found in the graves of the pagan Anglo-Saxons. I have dug up hundreds of them. Nearly all the glass ones appear to react to the 17 inch rate for Germany. In Christian times the Anglo-Saxons wore much smaller strings of beads, little drum-shaped things for the most part and of opaque red, green and occasionally yellow or blue glass. There are also some quite large beads like spindle-whorls an inch or so across. About half of the large beads are of opaque cobalt blue with white or yellow bands inlaid. Another group, however, are of clear green or amethyst colour, inlaid with threads of blue and white mosaic glass in the manner of Edinburgh, or Torquay, rock. These I had always believed to have been made in Ireland.

Here the results were a surprise. None of the little beads responded to the (pagan Anglo-Saxon) German rate (17), but to that of France (21). The large opaque beads appeared to be German, and the clear glass mosaic ones (the 'snake beads' of older archaeologists) were, it seems, French. There were no Irish beads at all. If this is correct, then the pendulum has much to say in the archaeology to come. From perhaps the seventh century onwards French glass seems to have ousted the products of the German Rhineland. It is interesting too to observe that opaque turquoise-grey 'melon' beads made of faïence, which are found occasionally in pagan Anglo-Saxon graves and frequently in the remains of Roman Britain, react to the 10 inch rate for Italy. Of course this is far too big a subject to bother about here. Anglo-Saxon crystal beads, amethyst beads and 'magic' balls appear to have come from India (5), and amber from Norfolk.

Beads of any kind are not frequently found on medieval sites in Britain, but I did once pick up a small, clear, yellow glass one on the site of the vanished medieval town of Kenfig in Glamorgan. I gave this to Horace Beck, the great expert and classifier of beads, who thought it was medieval. He also believed that the black beads from Cul na Croise belonged to the Viking Age. So little is really known that the pendulum could easily prove to be the clearest guide.

I tried two counts on different days for each specimen. One for the date of manufacture and one for that of its loss. Of course it was not expected that the dates of manufacture would agree closely. There are many factors which would go into the composition of a necklace, and they are obvious in many of the strings of beads we find in Anglo-Saxon graves. The beads may have come from different glass works and have been made at very different times. Then they were probably transported in bulk and made up into strings perhaps by some pedlar's wife. Any bead may get into a particular necklace and its purchaser may have added old beads of her own.

But if the necklace breaks and the beads are lost, this will happen in one minute. We would expect therefore very different results from the two tables of pendulum readings and this is what we do find. The possible error of a year at either end of the count remains as before:

Pendulum Estimate of the Dates of Nine Glass Beads

Type of Bead	Date of Manufacture	Date of Loss
Clear yellow, ovoid, brambled	A.D. 998	A.D. 1063
Opaque black, disc	993	1063
Clear cobalt blue, polygonal	989	1064
Clear yellow, disc	989	1063
Clear white, polygonal	1006	1063
Opaque black, spherical	980	1064
Opaque black, spherical	1026	1062
Clear yellow, ovoid	1033	1063
Opaque black, spherical	996	1063
	Average A.D. 1063	

The difference between these two tables is clear at once, and it seems obvious that while the beads were made at different dates they were all lost, if we make allowances for the difficulty in observation, in the same year. They were presumably all part of one necklace, which broke in the year A.D. 1063.

It is useless to try this method with mass produced objects. Nothing has passed to them from the mind of the maker. This can be shown easily by trying to find the dates of modern, or even Roman coins. The pendulum can perhaps date the time of loss, but not the year of production. I am afraid this may cause disappointment to many experimenters who do not know it. Beads, of course, were shaped by hand and then worn by somebody. They are in quite a different category. It is not the object which has its own impressions. This only retains those forced by somebody's mind into its own particular 'field'. How much this field may retain can be seen by the following extract from a letter to me by a lady to whom I had told this way of finding dates:

April 4th, 1968.

... I went to tea in Chalfont St Peter with someone who is also interested in dowsing. She has a thirteen year old son who collects odd bits and pieces and has a garden shed for his odds and ends. I found age rates for a doll's head (1920), the lid off a snuff box, brass (1901), and a small terra cotta statue (1876). Then we noticed it was marked '1876' inside the hollow end. It thrilled me that I was right ...

Then I tried over a rusty piece of iron, flat with two holes punched in it. It was flaking with age and had broken, jagged ends. This went on and on. I got to 380 (i.e. A.D. 1588) and had something happen. I was looking at a line of people, dressed very oddly, straggling behind four others who were carrying a large chest on their shoulders. In front walked three people, one in front and the other two behind. And I smelled the sweet scent of gorse on a hot day. It faded and I found I was still counting. At 503 (A.D. 1465) it stopped. My hostess said quickly 'Are you all right?' I sat down on a box feeling very, very sick. I never told her. But what did I see? It would be 1465, give a year here or there. The picture was as though I was watching a strip of film.

Yours sincerely,
Violet Beresford.

Now others have written describing their successes with this method of finding dates, but Mrs Beresford has gone much further. She has combined dowsing with psychometry and apparently obtained a picture of a past happening with an exact date attached. Her picture began at 380 turns, which represents A.D. 1588. Could it be that she was actually seeing something which happened in the Armada year? The ironwork was apparently made in the reign of Edward IV, but the procession perhaps took place in the days of Queen Elizabeth and the Spanish invasion threat.

Of course, this is a most important piece of information. Dowsing has already become an art, used in both peace and war; but it has been regarded as being in quite a different category from psychometry, that is, the art of reading impressions from objects, which is usually looked upon as the very doubtful prerogative of professional soothsayers. Here, however, in this case of Mrs Beresford's experience, it is clear that dowsing and psychometry are part of the same faculty. If one is to be trusted, so is the other. We know that dowsing can produce concrete results. It seems as if we must accept psychometry also. We know that telepathy works. Here now are three facets of one faculty which Victorian science regarded as childish superstition. All of them can be shown to work, and not only do they work, but there seems to be no limit to the manner of their working. It affects the whole way in which we regard man's mental make-up.

It is not the trivial things we are able to find beneath the grass which matter, nor the scraps of film, which we are able to see. The great point is that something in man's make-up is independent of space, time and the five senses. It seems difficult to avoid the conclusion that another part of us lives in a different world, where such things as limit us on earth no longer exist.

Notes on Pendulum Rates

This subject is vast and it is becoming clear to me that everything, whether subjective or objective, has a series of co-ordinates classifying it. If I attempted to find and tabulate all, the result would be more elaborate than the London telephone directory. I will give one example, and leave other people to work out more for themselves, although I will follow up the example with a table of rates which give you the first part of the series of co-ordinates.

At the beginning of *A Step in the Dark* I told the story of a rare little beetle called *Bolboceras armiger*, and how in 1964 it led us to a search for truffles with the pendulum. In the course of this quest another beetle, *Serica brunnea*, came into the story, a snail, *Cyclostoma elegans*, a truffle, *Sclerogaster compactus*, and the beech tree, *Fagus sylvatica*. These various organisms all responded to a rate of 17 inches. I could not find an imago of *Serica brunnea* for four years, and then on 2 August 1968 I found one lying on the window sill of the same bedroom in which I had formerly discovered the specimen of *Bolbocera armiger*, which had started the whole thing off.

This seemed a good opportunity to see how far one could get with the study of classifying co-ordinates. I knew that when on the right rate, the pendulum would make a given number of gyratory turns, or revolutions, for a given object or thought concept. Then it went back into an oscillation. This I knew was used by some dowsers for some purpose of which I was not very clear. However, I decided to count the number of oscillations and see what story they might tell. The answer with these five differing specimens is given in the table at top of opposite page.

All are evidently tied to the beech tree itself, on whose products they feed.

It was obvious that the new oscillatory reading could not be observed with complete certainty to nearer than two, or perhaps three swings, but, beyond that margin of error, it was correct. Making allowance for this 2 per cent margin, it becomes clear that the figures in the oscillation column are a multiple of the 'rate' by some number which differs

Name of Species	Rate	No. of Revolutions	No. of Counter-Revolutions	No. of Oscillations
Serica brunnea	17	17	150	17
Bolboceras armiger	17	17	171	17
Sclerogaster compactus	17	17	180	17
Fagus sylvatica	17	17	205	17
Cyclostoma elegans	17	17	280	17

according to the species concerned. The column should read: 17 × 9, 17 × 10, 17 × 10½, 17 × 12 and 17 × 16; that is 153, 170, 178½, 204 and 282. We are clearly a step forward in finding out part of a vast system of classification, which includes everything. There must be many more co-ordinating numbers to find. But, once again I must stress that whoever compiled this table did so on a scale of inches, which is human measurement. The mind working on these figures works in a human manner. Whatever we are dealing with is susceptible to human reasoning, even if it reflects the mentality of somebody on a higher plane of development than our own. It is not a product of my mind (even though I suspected that it might be) for others get precisely the same results as I do. We are forced to assume elaborate planning outside normal earth life. When once this fact is grasped, enormous strides in knowledge are possible. I am only a pioneer.

A Table of Rates

1	1½	2	3	3½	4
			Rosemary	Lavender	Currant
Congo	Zambia				

4½	5	5½	6	7	8
Bramble	Rose	May Phosphorous	Ash	Memory Sulphur	Flesh Carrion
				Brown Scent	Silphadae
	India				Libya
	Nigeria		Persia	Egypt	Morocco

9	9½	10	10½	11	12
Elder		EAST			
Chlorine	Nitrogen	Fire			
			Ivy	Oak	Cherry
Purple			Walnut		
Safety	Psi	Graphite			Carbon
		Milk			
Israel		Red			Orange
		Light			Disease
		Sun		*Lucanidae*	Pride
		Youth			
		Man			
		Bulgaria		Yugoslavia	
		Italy		Spain	
				Portugal	

12½	13	13⅜	13½	14	15
	Rowan				
Mercury				Silica	
		Length	Voice		
	Greece			Russia	Poland
				Hungary	Turkey

16	17	18	19½	20
				SOUTH
Grass	Beech	Apple		Earth
				Electricity
				White
Dung				Heat
Sex				Love
Scarabs				Life
Austria	Finland	China	Denmark	Belgium
E. Germany	W. Germany			Holland

$20\frac{1}{2}$	21	$21\frac{1}{2}$	22	$22\frac{1}{2}$
Hazel		Magnetism		
	Potassium		Lead	Magnesium
			Silver	
			Sodium	
			Calcium	
	Fungi	Scotland	Grey	
N. Ireland		Channel Is.	England	
	I. of Man	Ireland	Wales	
	France			
	Switzerland			

23	24	25	26	$26\frac{1}{2}$	$26\frac{2}{3}$
Elm					
	Diamond	Aluminium	Alcohol		Oxygen
	Male				Thickness
Sweden				Canada	
Norway				S. Africa	

27	28	29	$29\frac{1}{2}$	30	$30\frac{1}{2}$
				WEST	
Garlic	Yew			Water	
Thought	Tin	Gold		Hydrogen	Copper
		Yellow		Green	Cobalt
Stink		Danger	Minus Psi	Sound	Blue
				Moon	
		Female		Age	
U.S.A.			Australia		

31	32	33	$33\frac{1}{2}$	34	35
Pine	Violet			Cypress	
	Iron				
	Aspirin				
			New Zealand		

36	37	38	39	40/0
Evolution		Tomato	Potato	NORTH Air
				Black Cold
				Breadth Anger Deceit Sleep Death

As I said before, I am only giving the 'rates', the first of the co-ordinates. The table is quite rudimentary and gives little more than a 150th of these. In reality it should contain every concept known to man. However it will serve as a starting point for other investigators and contains much that is fundamental to life. Above all it demonstrates the importance of the four cardinal points at the four quarters of the forty divisional circle. Everything is linked to the earth's mass and not to its magnetic field.

Index

Index

For Product Safety Concerns and Information please contact our EU
representative GPSR@taylorandfrancis.com
Taylor & Francis Verlag GmbH, Kaufingerstraße 24, 80331 München, Germany